COLORS WASH OVER ME

POEMS BY LOWCOUNTRY STUDENTS, VOLUME ONE
2021-2022

FREE VERSE PRESS
A FREE VERSE, LLC EXPERIENCE

1

This publication and the POETS IN SCHOOLS program
were made possible by the Academy of American Poets
with funds from the Andrew W. Mellon Foundation.

poets.org
mellon.org
poetsinschools.com

*Poets in
Schools*

ISBN: 978-1-7374696-5-0

Library of Congress Control Number: 2022938683

Book design by Marcus Amaker

Printed in the United States of America.

First printing edition 2022

Published by Free Verse Press
Free Verse, LLC
Charleston, South Carolina

freeversepress.com

TABLE OF CONTENTS

7. Angel Oak Elementary

12. Buist Academy

48. Burke High School

56. The Charleston Catholic School

84. East Cooper Montessori School

91. James Island Charter High School

96. Laing Middle School

108. Moultrie Middle School

134. North Charleston Creative
     Arts Elementary

156. Palmetto Scholars Academy

164. Sanders-Clyde Creative
Arts Elementary School

176. Eugene Sires
Elementary School

186. Wando High School

220. Whitesville Elementary

DEAR READERS,

Doing a book like this became my dream when I was named the first Poet Laureate of Charleston in 2016. That's when I stepped up my work in schools and did a lot of research on the best ways to draw creativity out of students.

Young scholars have taught me so much. I am in awe of their honesty, humor, and humility. You'll see a lot of their spirit in these poems.

This book absolutely could not have happened without the support of the Academy of American Poets. This collection was made possible by the Academy with funds from the Andrew W. Mellon Foundation.

And this book absolutely could not have happened without the local poets who went into classrooms and came away with an inbox full of poems: Evelyn Berry, Marjory Wentworth, Asiah Mae, Chelsea Grinstead, Will Davis, and Yvette Murray.

Read more about this book and the Poets in Schools program at poetsinschools.com

This is the first of many collections. Thank you for reading. Support young voices!

— Marcus Amaker

ANGEL OAK ELEMENTARY

TEACHER: TIM HOECKEL
POET INSTRUCTOR: MARCUS AMAKER
5TH GRADE

When I listen to music,
It gets my body moving,
Hands clapping,
Feet tapping,
Music makes me move,
Singing songs that have good sounds,
Music makes my day,
Music makes my frown,
Go upside down,
The tempo of my heart goes fast
When I listen to music.

— Rashard C.
5th Grade

My Playlist

I walk along the street,
Walking to the beat.

The lyrics appear in my mind,
Filled with rhymes.

I hum as I go around, about, along, and away.

The song changes and I pause,
Please play another, is that really a bother?

It's fine,
I guess.

I walk along the street,
Walking to the beat.

— Camden M.
5th Grade

Rap, I sit back ,
With my backpack,
With the tapes in there,
And when I get home,
I hit the snare,
Because I need to share it,
With my instructor,
I feel like I'm in a blockbuster.

— Davis C.
5th Grade

My Poem

Music makes me dance,
Music bring me happiness,
I could jam to jolly jingles of joy,
When I listen I can't stop,
Then the beat drops,
Let's pop,
Music makes me dance,
I start to flow,
In my head I glow,
I stand out of the crowd,
Then things get loud,
I can feel the power,
I can listen when I shower,
I can feel the power.

— Josephine C.
5th Grade

Beat Seat

Music is like the beat in my seat,
I get out of my beat seat and dance,
When I get tired of my dance chance,
I get down and sing,
It's like a ring in my ear,
That calms me down,
I nod my head in my nodding beat seat.

— Emily M.
5th Grade

When I listen to music,
It is like musicians in my ears,
I think of all the musicians I could think of,
Music is my life
Music is life,
Music helps everyone.

— Christopher W.
5th Grade

When I hear my sound,
My fingers hit the strings,
Play that sorta thing,
It makes my heart beat.

I fill up with music,
To the tip of my tongue,
I feel the beat rising,
I want to sing that song.

— Susanna W.
5th Grade

BUIST
ACADEMY

TEACHER: **MRS. KARLIEN EISEMAN**
POET INSTRUCTOR: **MARCUS AMAKER**
5TH GRADE

Music is like a relieving scream

When I listen to music It's like
I relax and I dream

The sound of happiness is the sound
of magic it is very enthusiastic

A good song is like (littomy
music to my ears
People react, they dance, sing,
and also shed tears.

Cameron C.

To me, music is magic.
The flow of the song
It's like a dashing.

The sound sways soorning through.
It has its ups and downs too.
Now The best kind conserves kindness.

To me, music is magic.
The flow of the song.
Sometimes, has calness.

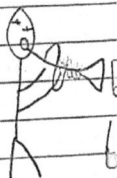

Music is Magic.

Jordan J.

Music is like a mystery tone. It can be as loud as a lightning strike or music can be as quiet as a drop of water.

Jayden Z.

Shubha K.

When I play the piano, the music swirls. Green, blue, orange yellow, silver and gold. I let the colors wash over me, my fingers dancing on the keyboard. When I play, nobody can break me out of my colorful bubble.

When the violin plays, I watch the pinks, and soft greens, and buttery yellows. I see the violin pull the musician up in an ocean of music. The sea pulls me up too. There is nothing that can break us from the flow.

The drums rock me, shake me, pounding and throbbing. It's blacks, reds, and bright blues, and yellow hues sweep it's message into my brain. It pushes me higher and higher, bursting out of the clouds, and breaking all the boundries.

Colors everywhere as I drift down, and then colors slowly, sleepily, drift away, revealing a true power, meant to be shared.

Music

Mya B.

Music is like magic.
The energy in the air.
The life it brings.

Music is like mist.
Slowly spreads to everyone.
Unforgetable.

Music is meaningful.
Each song having a diffrent meaning.
Diffrent story.

Music has its own mind.
You can't control its words.
It plays itself.

♪♫♪♫♪♫♫♪♫

When I listen to music my heart lifts
my worries fly to the
sky. The song fills my head
with the happiest thought.
It flows through my brain
as inspiration goes.
It makes me leap
and dance all day
My heart leaps as
my talent grows
at the end of the
song my talent
has been known.
And my only
word was this
dance
dance
dance

Hazel B

magical
MUSIC
By: Maddrey

When I press play
I pretend to play the
pretty song.

Maddrey M.

My name is Maddrey
and music is magnificent.
When it plays it
makes me perfect.

I pretend to sing the
wonderful, beautiful
song.

Music is music to
my ears. It lets
me let loose to
the groove.

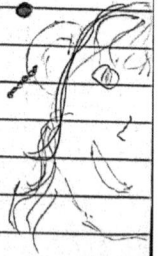

Sometimes I find they
make me happy. That
makes me get so
sappy.

The beautiful song
goes bong bong bong.
Then I decide to
sing along.

Brogan M.

Music is like a singing voice
from tech, or in real life.
From rock to rap does not matter,
It still is good like whatever it
is. From a baby singing cocomelon
to NBA M singing rap god. It
does not matter what it
is but it is good. When I listen
to rap the words go through
my ears like food digesting
through my body. Music is like
your cat who is always
hungry. Music is like all of
the air flowing in a
indoor colliseum. Does not matter
what it is it is still good.

air
baseball
field
giant
Collisen

Braelynn W.

When i listen to Music, that calming tune puts me
in a calm Mood. A calm song is like peace that
never went wrong. A lovely song is like fresh
cool air in the breeze, putting me at ease,
Its like the hearing of rain on a stormy night.
Music to me is calming like the sound of swishing
Ocean water on a beach.

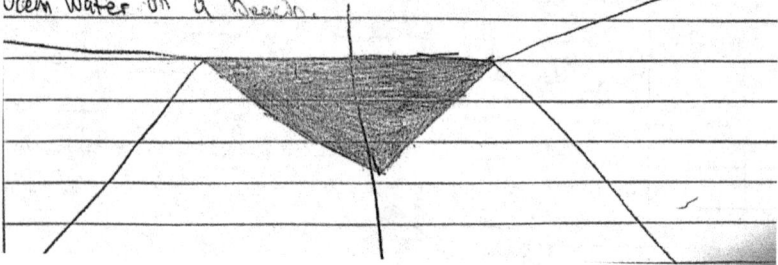

Cheyenne **P.**

Four
stanzas

Music

Music can lead to many things
You can hate it or love, we wont judge
Musicshians use math to steady a good beat
so you'll dance with your feet.

Your favorite song is on the radio
how do feel, do you dance, sing or move
around. Music can be things you
wouldn't suspect, it could be waves
whistling in the oceans or the sound
of feet tapping on a slower beat.

Music is like a gift to my
ears, but if close your eyes you can
imainige what you hear. Do you
hear birds chirping is that what you
hear or do you like chainsaws when
they turn on is that a gift to you.
Maybe you like the sound of bell jingling
on your favorite christmas music.

Music can be your comfort, Just like you like to slumber. You can't control it even if you try to hold it. You might meet your favorite artist, saying your job looks so easy they say. You only like it because it please you, you might think an artist is superior than others like Nicki Manjai is over Cardi B. Maybe it's the Lyrics or the rythem, that makes you top with a beat.

Ayla J.

Music is like a soft rain pattering in my mind. , Running through my head until I know every line. Music protects me from the sounds of the world, from the people fighting to the people crying I try to block it out for with a click of the play button I can drown it all out.

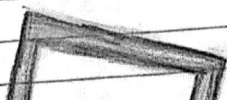

Music to me is like a perfect illusions personified plant that runs though the breeze. Music to me is like a loving little bird going to see it's momma. Muis is sweet like candy. Music is perfect like imperfections. Music is so good it makes me complete. Music can calm me down or cheer me up, thats why i love music. I wana listen to music all the time music to me is just sublime. That's why i love music

Evelin C.

"What a song does" By Finleigh
Does a song make you sing
Does a song make you dance
Does a song make you smile
even when the sun doesn't
shine

Will a song make you sing,
even when your blue

Not singing a song
is like stopping at a
stop light

Then when you sing again
you move foward and
never look back to singing
a sad song

Finleigh A.

Mimi

Music

Music makes me fly away
The second that it starts to play
I go to a colorful special place
Music puts a smile on my face
Music can make your emotion change
It can make you sad, scared, happy, angry
and everything inbetween
You can sing a sad short song
Or just listen and dance along
You can write your own music
Making each line special
Music is in your body in your home
Just listen

Mimi Y.

Music makes me feel...
like a bird with wings
soaring into the sky,
an airplane that is free
to fly, a student who
dosen't have to try lie,
someone who feels like
they don't have to
try.

Julia B.

Music is... like a dog
that barks, powerfull
and brave even in the
dark.

Music can sound...
powerfull yet sad even
at the same time,
though we say its all
different could we all
be the same?

Ryhming Words

Music comnnects us
in all different ways.

-try -dark
-fly -bark
-lie
-sky
-bye
-shy

29

when music starts playing, my hands start swaying. Even if it only is through my head it always gets me go to bed.

Music is ryhme, ny them, and rap.
Music is poetry, pizza, and pop.
Music is in my mind my head phones my speaker.

Music is everywhere.

noah P.

Makai's poem

Makai S.

I feel happy
I feel hopeful
I feel some hatred
I feel Human
I feel like bones and
someone chewing

H = alliteration
I feel = repetion
bones & chewing = Rhyme

When I listen to music I break
down on the ground and then
I get an bed after putting on
a goune I rhyme all the time
and I am Makai.

31

Inspiration into instruments   by Henry BP

Music is like a bird that soars
Music is like the opening of doors
Music is like the end of wars.
Inspiration born anew.

An idea flowed from inspiration, then an invention, an
instrument, another idea. Hip hop, blues, jazz, classical, too.
Every type has a time when it's over.

Inspiration, idea, invention. Poetry, writing, books. Hand
in hand, into music.

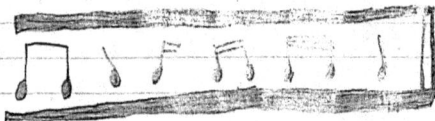

Henry B.P.

music is nature and trees and
the sound of the river rushing as the
robin in its nest sings a sweet
song
music is that party across the street
has you lie in your bed
music is the movie that you watch before
your eyes start to get heavy.
music is in the city as you walk
by the band you hear Christmas song
as you think about what to buy in the
store for your friend.
Musk is everywhere you just have to
listen.

by Henrys

Henry S.

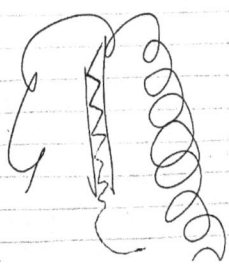

When day becomes night
and the stars start to shine
the music of the earth is loud in my mind
The music sounds like my mothers soft words
her accent ringing in my ear leaving a whisper
the sound of music is special to me
because it means I am free.
When morning comes I hear the soft
sound of birds up above.
singing to me a special song
saying everythings going to be all right
saying I love you from high up above.

Lil P.

M₂

Samara

Samara N.

I awake to the sound of birds singing
a harmony, singing a song that's special
to me. Tweet, tweet, tweet.

Some cars go by beeping a harmony, beeping
a song that's special to me. Beep, beep,
beep.

Music is beautiful. Music is art. Music is life
Music is easy, make a song and don't
even try, All you need is a beat to
start, make sure that you sing from the
heart.

Music and poetry, are exactly the same,
poetry and music have only one name.

ART

Cale 11/29/21

Cale N.   ~~MUSIC~~   Blue birds.

Music is like blue birds singing.
When the day is ending the birds go (away)
then they come out in the very next (day)
They come with joy and their ready to
Play. But, when the day turns dawn they will
say were coming back there next day,
Blue birds birds burst from the field
and yell and play while the people want
them to go away. The people don't like
them to sing and play while the birds,
Just want to stay and not go away.

Hank 5C

Hank B.

Music is like a pounding river circling round the lines. Some times it is slow like a sloth. Some times music is fast faster than a fire.
Some times it goes around a normal pace wondering place to place.

The Sound of the Keys

Marie B.

The sound of the keys as I press
them down each makes a different
sound

When I play the notes together they
make a sounds full of wonder
takes me to a dream that
opeans up me a let my feelings
into a world were they will wonder

Each little note put on a paper
there is a word that gose under
and bounces off the wall
and down the hall
as I sing it loud and proud
as it is in tune with the note
above

The song stays there to cheer me
on as the day gose on
It keeps me going through the
day until I got back to play
again

Hippopotamus
by Jason S.

The sound of music is the sound of hippos
The loud snorting of their noses
As they splash into puddles making ripples
And then stomp away to another puddle

Their big teeth chomp on stuff
And don't share with any other hippo
Soon they slowly swallow the chewy meat
The meat is chewy so it's quite a feat

The sound they make as they chew
is weird and squishy and sounds good

Music is a like the life to my day. Music brights my day with the blah blah blah blah. My ears hear heavily doy when I listen to music. My hearts gos to the beat of music. Although people don't music my heart loves the songs it goes fast.

Music is like a good day at
a show
I'm happy when I listen to music
I'm happy when I ride Blaze,

The Sounds are like my Sadle
& the beat is my bridle

I have the music in my head not
the reins

The sound is the pound o the
canter to a jump

Gray H.

Music is like _____ ~~...inson~~ ⟶

Music is like

waking up to   **Elzie A.**
the smell of bacon,
wafting through the air,
all the way to your
room and it touches your nostril hair.
Music is like the way that
the taste of warm hot cocoa
sits in your mouth, even when
you breathe in and out.
Music is like the sounds of
birds chirping, the sound stuck
in your ear. But when you wake up,
it's all you want to hear.
The way it makes you laugh.
The way it makes you cry.
The way it makes you want to listen
to it all night.

The sound of joy is the sound of R and B
my feet sweep of the floor when I hear
the beautiful, brilliant sounds of R and B. I
fly, fly, fly to the sky when I hear the amazing
awesome sounds of R and B. I love the
taste of the great base. The base of
the music is what I taire. I taire it
into my soul of light make one of my
own songs? ___ I might. I JUST might

Ryleigh W.

"The silent sounds"

Riley SC

The sounds of music makes us move
with the beat of the silent sounds and
tense when the silent sound is not silent
anymore and becomes a cacophony of gracefulness
rushing through our ears.

Riley C.

When i liston to music i makes
me feel good.When i liten to music
it helps. my headphones sing to me
When i press play, music make me
feel like my self. A good song
is like getting a new dog

Frankie B.

Music is how you feel in the moment.
If you are sad you will listen to a sad guitar,
or maybe a light piano.
Or if you happy you will listen to pop or rap.
It may go from Olivia Rodrigo to Bethovenor
Travis Scott to Taylor Swift.
But music is more about the
sensation and the vibration.

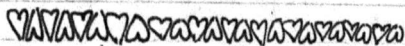

Lydia M.

BURKE HIGH SCHOOL

TEACHER: DEBORAH CARICO
POET INSTRUCTOR: ASIAH MAE
9TH – 12TH GRADE

'Round midnight Monk plays.
Black hat on black hair above black hands on white keys
playing black music
for an audience that doesn't understand,
or thinks they do.
Glares at the piano and the sound turns around,
frowns at the bass and it starts to walk,
talks to himself. Lips drawn tight and thin.
The song ends. Handkerchiefs are pulled out to mop
slick brows. Another begins.

— Adam V.
11th Grade

Memories Shared

This happiness it consumes me.
The way the lyrics be.
The music that hurts.
The music that cries.
The music that burns with unbridled rage.

The happiness that isn't my own.
These tears that call my eyes home,
Sparkling like cider falling,
Striking dawny softness.

It isn't fair how they control.
My heart takes these heavy hits with a toll,
Listening to the pain,
Listening to the experience,
Listening to the moment I never wished to experience.

Each tear from my eyes applause.
Every line of lyrics a claw
Tearing tanned hide,
Tearfully.

— Ty'Lynn S.
12th Grade

I am silent.
I wonder if I found my voice,
how I would change the world.
I hear that silent people don't get anything done,
Yet I see the opposite.
I want to break out of my cocoon of silence,
make an impact;
And yet, I am silent.

I pretend to have it all together,
everything under control.
I feel cluttered.
Like the family junk drawer in the kitchen;
so full up I can hardly open.
I touch the illusion of serenity I've created,
the mask of calm.
I worry my clutter will make me unsuccessful.
I cry when the drawer won't open. Something's stuck
and I can't get it out.
I am silent.

I understand my best is *the* best.
I say "I know" and "I'm confident,"
And I dream to believe that.
I try to believe that.
I hope to better my best. A relentless, ruthless regimen
of training.
I am silent.

— Alyrah H.
9th Grade

Words

I listen to the masters and struggle to replicate sound in a musical culture that rejects imitation.

I pause Montgomery's solos and fiddle with a tone knob, then mangle what I just heard.

His Gibson can make notes whisper, shout, mutter, hum and sing.

Baritone, alto, and tenor all meld together.

My guitar chews on the notes, dislikes the taste of rhythm, and burps out a glob of sonic mess.

I checked my phone , switched on mute since practice began. 12:07. It's been an hour since I started.

"It don't mean a thing if it ain't got that swing!"

Yeah, I know. Thanks, Ellington.

— Adam V.
11th Grade

Victory On the Scale

The struggles of life weigh heavy on her body.
She knew that it was time for a change.
Living day to day with different emotions, because her
self confidence was lost
deep in the ocean.
She knew in her mind self-love needed to be found,
so her journey was now revealed,
deep in the ground.
Her struggles of life lessons,
as she embraces her blessings.
With the help of her family,
Her confidence arose once more.
Day one.
Day one felt like weights were being held
on her shoulders,
forcing herself away.
from the smell of deep-fried chicken.
And the sweet taste of sweet tea.
She felt like she was in heaven but,
she stopped.
An image popped into her mind, a girl.
A sweet little girl.
Who believed she could achieve her dream.
She came back into reality and looked at the delicious
meal once more.
And she threw it away.

— Trinitee G.
11th Grade

I Love

I love her as she loves me
She doesn't hurt me like the others did
She treats me with the careful firmness of a master
craftsmen
She's so tooth achingly sweet
I feel as though I'll break when she touches,
so vulnerable I feel
Watching her laugh and smile fills me with campfire
warmth
With gooey softness that melts everywhere
So we sit and love

I love him as he loves me
He is my glue
Just as I am his
A viscosity that promises eternal longevity
Firm chains of safety
That pull and touch and reach
He is my crutch as much as I am his
A steel rod tied to a sapling so it remains sturdy
So we sit and love

I love them as they love me
All consuming storms that swallow me whole
There is no comparisons
How do you compare the sun and moon?
Both so ethereal, stories will remain forever
Both my loves are equal in power and strong
So I pray to the sun and the moon
That we will always be okay
And even if we aren't, our pinkies never untwine
So we sit and love.

— Ty'Lyn S.
12th Grade

THE CHARLESTON CATHOLIC SCHOOL

TEACHER: **MRS. DONNA CLEARY**
POET INSTRUCTOR: **MARCUS AMAKER**
5TH GRADE

Kim clicked and clapped as he enter the basement
And he didn't find what he was looking for
Binging and Banging he did not find
what he was looking for
He hoped and hoped that he would find it
Fumbling and flailing he finally found it

— Henry A.
5th Grade

The Big Beat Battle

Lit the lighthouse
lit a light to find a bee to beat in a beat battle.
The big blue bee Breet was going for a treat and then
she hit a brilliant beat to beat the little Lit the light-
house. The little Lit the lighthouse thought that was not
so neat to try to hit a beat. So Lit lit his lighthouse with
a light and the light was so bright it blinded the big blue
bee Breet and that is how Lit the lighthouse beat Breet
the bee in a beat battle.

— Coltyn C.
5th Grade

Tank the Truck

Tank the truck's job is to pick up muck
Tank went to town to pick up muck
But then he realized it was too much muck to pick up
Then, his friend Buck the duck came to help him pick
up the muck
Buck came to town to help tank,
the truck pick up the mushy muck.
Together they had much luck and they finished picking
up muck.

— Vanessa G.
5th Grade

Rapper the Rat

Rapper was a rat, a rookie runner rat.
He ran a rookie race and rammed into a rainbow,
the rainbow was made and made it rain and rain and
rain, the runners got wet, and ran at Rapper, they all
rammed into a roof.

— Carmen W.
5th Grade

Daffodil

You look up at the sorrowful sky
Asking yourself a simple question,
You wonder, "How many stars are in the sky?"
You wonder how many wishes those stars
held.
How many people trusted those stars
to hold their secrets.
You tried to find a star that hadn't
already been held by a strong
secret. As you were standing there,
searching for
a helpful hand, the stars began
to fade into the darkness.
Then it hit you, you've been standing there
searching for stars all this
time, but you never needed one.
All you needed was someone
to listen.
Not someone to open their mouths,
But for someone to open their ears.
But now, all those people are gone
because you were too scared of
losing something much more valuable than a star.

— Catherine R.
5th Grade

Red

You can only have that feeling once.
You can only dream of that feeling once.
When you have that feeling don't ever let it go.
Because having the courage of letting someone into
your heart is saying a lot.
Having someone hold your heart in their trusting
palm, doesn't mean they will let you bleed all over it.
It means they will hold you until you cannot hold
yourself.
And when you cannot hold yourself...
Well, neither can they.
Thus, that feeling is over, because you couldn't bear
the truth of understanding that all good feelings come
to an end.

  — Catherine R.
5th Grade

When It Comes

It will beat, oh how it will beat!
While you stand still on the shallow hill.
While you breathe through your blissful lungs.
Then everything goes black.
You blink breathlessly, trying to understand
what just happened.
You rise brushing off the dust and
debris.
The brewing sound of blastful bombs
boomed in your bright ears.
You felt your heartbeat... beat... beat...
Oh the benevolent sound of your blooming heart!
Oh the beautiful, breathing lungs you
love so dearly!
But barring the sadness of knowing
nothing can ever stay perfect
you built yourself up,
brushing off the blackened tears
and bruised spirit,
but not letting it blind your beauty.
But being the only visible person there,
You broke your gaze and
returned to your blue earth.
Then, you heard it.
But only if we ever knew what was
lying in your head that day.
If only you lived to tell.

– Catherine R.
5th Grade

This poem is about all the lives lost in Ukraine. My heart goes to everyone who is suffering during these times.

Bitter Bill's Bitter Bread

Bitter Bill bought bread at the Boar's bread, but the bread was not bitter so he gave it to his big brother Non Bitter Brad. Then Non Bitter Brad ate the bread in his backyard. After that Bitter Bill bought more bread at a different store called the Big Boy Bakery, but it still wasn't bitter so he gave it to his back door neighbor Bashful Bill, his baby brother. Then for the third time Bitter Bill went to a different store called the big bashful boring bitter bread store and bought more bread but this time Bitter Bill's bread was bitter so Bitter Bill made his bitter bread sandwich.

— Dylan H.
5th Grade

Big Ben
Bought Big
Bright Blue Blocks
To Build Big
Bright Blue Buildings.

— William N.
5th Grade

Dancing Dreams

Dolphins dived in the deep.
The ocean's depth was dark and depressing.
Danny a dolphin was depressed but,
Dreams danced in Danny's head.
Danny was delighted and,
Danny, a dolphin, danced delightedly.
Dolphins in Danny's pod danced with him.
In the end, Danny and his dolphins danced delightedly.

– Presley W.
5th Grade

Windy Wall Street

Wendy watched the window,
Twas windy,
She wanted to walk to Wall Street,
When Wendy walked to Wall Street,
Rain and wind pushed her,
She was wrong,
She wouldn't walk to Wall Street,
With all that wind
Wendy watched Willbur wind his water wall,
When Willbur and Wendy met wally,
Wally was a walrus,
" Well Farewell " Wally whined,
They wondered how in the wonderful world he got here,
Then he left them in the Windiest Wall street in the
World wondering wonderful thoughts.

– Tolly G.
5th Grade

Perry's Plant

Perry buys a pot
She plants a pack of peppers
Throughout the years the pack of peppers started to
grow
But Perry soon noticed
That the pack of peppers weren't peppers at all
The pack of peppers was just a plant
Perry was blue
But still cared carefully for the plant

– Haven S.
5th Grade

Thomas the Train

Thomas the train thought about school; he loved
school. But then Thomas thought school would think
that Thomas thought that school was bad but Thomas
thought that school was really good because it made
him think good thoughts. Thomas was a good train and
he was glad that his title was Thomas the train.

– Matthew R.
5th Grade

Perseverance

As the drops trickled down, the clouds burst aloud, the thunder struck like a truck blowing up, as the cup filled with drops the rainbow struck the sky with the sun by its side!

– Sawyer-Gray M.
5th Grade

I got some pickled beets,
but the pickled beets were prickly,
so I went to the pickled store and got some of Bobby's beets,
then I ate them and they weren't prickly beets anymore.

– Jackson V.
5th Grade

Brown Eyes

Brown eyes wear crowns but when they look around they don't frown but if you frown you should turn it upside down and smile while you have brown eyes.

– Santana H.
5th Grade

Soaring Alone

I was sailing across the sea alone
I was staring into the night sky
Thinking about one small shooting star
It was alone
But shining so brightly
I wish I could be like that shooting star
Alone, soaring in space
But shining so brightly

– Julianne G.
5th Grade

The girl named Kate who would not skate
Kate would not skate she tried but all she did was say
I ate the skate then Tate came out and said hey Kate lets
go skate Kate said wait Tate I ate my skate sorry Tate.
Tate was sad and very mad, Tate asked Kate why the
skate you could have eaten my brother Nate. "But he's
too late," said Kate.

– Caroline S.
5th Grade

---

4 Kids

Pessy, Tessy, Jessy, and Lessy were very very messy,
they tried to clean but Pessy wouldn't help Tessy and
Tessy wouldn't help Jessy and Jessy wouldn't help
Lessy so their room stayed messy. PESSY, TESSY,
LESSY, JESSY, clean your room, said mama Fessy.

– Caroline S.
5th Grade

Hands

We are all better when we're together
When we are together we are stronger
Like our
Helping Hands

— Caroline S.
5th Grade

I see

I see the sun shine
With the radiant colors
of yellow and gold they are so bold
I see God's heart in my heart,
together we make someone new for you
I see the different colors of the dandelions in my
meadow that I made with my bare hands, ruby red,
burgundy, maroon and deep purple
I see butterflies in a cage covered with the green leaves
of nature that come alive when you nourish them
I can see but I can also hear the sound of beautiful
music, tuba in the distance, trombones up close, violin
and its harmony, guitar strings playing, a harp making
melody, we see, we hear, we smell and we taste all the
things surrounding us.

— Caroline S.
5th Grade

THE CHARLESTON CATHOLIC SCHOOL

TEACHER: **MRS. FARFONE**
POET INSTRUCTOR: **MARCUS AMAKER**
6TH GRADE

Birds Sing

When the birds sing a small light shows
But yet it grows and grows
Happiness spreads and things come to life
By the time the suns yawning humans are running
And there are many more clouds in the sky

— Sally T.
6th Grade

Greatness

Greatness forms in different ways
People think great is being good
And they try to take it by greediness
But the truth is gratitude and graciousness
Is how you become great and stay great
If you grip the idea that that greatness is easy to get
And sometimes you try greediness when really you need
gratitude
That's what you need to be great!

— Sally T.
6th Grade

Ukraine Fights Back

Ukraine Fights back
against Filthy Russia,
For while Zelensky Fought,
Putin stayed put in the middle of Russia,
having parties in his pristine palace.
The Ukrainian civilians took up forearms though,
with their hearts Filled with courage and strength,
they Fought those Filthy Russians back,
and while I may not know the Final results,
I know the Ukrainians who Fought,
Filled with courage and strength,
will always be Favored and victorious in my heart.

— Andres J.
6th Grade

Sally's Super Spiders

Sally says spiders are super
Cindy says she thinks differently
Cindy said she was super scared of spiders
Sally said she was scared of spiders too
she just thought they were splendid

— Anna G.
6th Grade

Cate, the Curious Cat

Cate, the Curious Cat had captured a cute caterpillar
Cate was confused by the caterpillar because of how it
climbed up the wall and clumsily fell down then Cate,
the Curious Cat had also tried to climb to climb and just
the same clumsily fell down after that Cate, the Curious
Cat wasn't confused why the cute caterpillar kept
clumsily falling down.

— Evan L.
6th Grade

The Book About a Crook

She had a book
the book was found in a nook
about a crook with a look
the crook cooked a hook
the hook tied and shook the crook with a look
and she finished the book

— Hannah E.
6th Grade

Anna Loves Appendix Horses

Anna loves appendix horses.
Anna loves to feed them apples.
Appendix horses love alfalfa.
Anna feeds them alfalfa.
Appendix horses love horses love apples and alfalfa.
Anna knows that some horses can't eat too much alfalfa.
Anna wants to know if all horses can have apples.
Anna wants to know if all horses can eat alfalfa.

— Anna W.
6th Grade

Another Day

Another day another day
what is another day to you
is another day just another way
to fall to lose to fail or get a bruise
although that may be what a day seems like to you
that is not what a day is to me
another day is another chance
a chance to live laugh and play
a chance to be better and a chance to pray
a chance to be great
a chance to be your true self
a chance to create something new
thats of your own design
and last but not least a chance to let your light shine
one thing I hope you will always do is think about how
you approach the day
and choose to approach it the happy way

— Phoebe H.
6th Grade

The Sad Reality

How I wished I was a bubble
dancing in the water
reaching for the top
until I came to the sad reality
that soon I would pop.

— Phoebe H.
6th Grade

The Race

Robin was jealous. His friend Robey could run really
fast, and I mean really fast. Robin wished that he could
run that fast. Robin wanted to beat Robey in a race
more than anything. Robin trained everyday to beat
Robey in a race. Robin ran many miles everyday. Robey
saw him running and said you can't beat me, never ever.
Robin challenged Robey to a race. Robin won the race
against Robey. Robey was in shock that Robin won the
race. Robey said how did you win that race. Robin said
with hard work and determination you can do anything.
Robey then went on to respect Robin everyday after
that one race. Robin then went on to win many more
races. People world wide respected and admired Robin.
All because of that one race.

— Tradd S.
6th Grade

Bella's Adventure

Bella chases birds,
but then she got hurt
and mom put Bella in her bedroom.

Bella decided to be brave and leave the house,
this time she caught a bunny.
She saved it for breakfast and ate it.

Then she fell asleep with a nice full belly for the day.

— Ryan T.
6th Grade

Nicholas

Better bruised
weak when winning
Strong fighter in any battle
The small and big
But of course on that cold November day the best battle
he fought came to an end.

— Caroline R.
6th Grade

Bob's Lunch

Bob was going to the butcher shop to get lunch, the butcher gave Bob the best beef that the butcher had in his store. But the butcher didn't realize Bob wanted the best brisket not the best beef so the butcher took back the beef and gave Bob the brisket. Then Bob took his brisket to his brown house and read a book while eating his brisket. Bob took a look at the book and said this is a good book while eating his brisket.

— Nathan B.
6th Grade

That smelly skunk had stank me up and stole my silly hat and stank that up oh dear oh dear I smell like fowl fungus strapped on that skunk.
Oh how I wish I could get this smell off.
Old Spice can help with this silly stanky smelly fungus skunk problem.

— Matthew S.
6th Grade

Clare and friends

Clare the cute dog went into the creek, while she was in the creek she realized she wanted her friends Connor and Cooper to come in the creek! Then she noticed she couldn't carry Cooper and Connor's collars! So she asked them to carry their collars, and Cooper and Connor got out of the creek and helped cute Clare.

— Ava D.
6th Grade

The big, black sea
was filled with beautiful
burrows of animals
with colors so
big and bright and bold.
And when I leave the big, black sea
I remember the big, bright, bold colors
and I long to go back
to the sea that was big
with the colors so bright
with the burrows of animals
that lived in the black sea.

— Isabella P.
6th Grade

When I listen to music
my whole life lights up.
My eyes fill with colors
and my mind fills with endless possibilities.
It's like my body is under a spell
It's like I was sick, but now I am well.
Music is my
       light,
          my
            life.
I can hear the different voices
and instruments, and I have so many choices.
Do I stay where I am? Do I follow my dream?
Can I be who I am?
Music answers these questions.
It fills my soul with hope and love
and I feel like nothing can go wrong,
If
  there's
      music.

— Isabella P.
6th Grade

Music is Everything

Music is everything.
Music is the sound of my flute,
 the clanging of metal,
 the clicking and sticking of the keys.
Music is the whistle of the first notes,
 my hopes that I make a sound.
Music is the height of happiness in my heart,
 the highest pitch on my instrument.
Music is sought, sung, and saw in many different ways.
Music is the melody I play in a band,
 the beat I feel forever like sand.
Music is everything.

— Anna C.
6th Grade

Sally's S'mores

Sally went to get a s'more,
But when Sally looked she had no more.
So Sally went to the store to get some s'mores,
But when she got to the store they had no more.
She kept on looking for the s'mores
Finally she found some more at the s'more store!

— Blair G.
6th Grade

The sun in the sky:
Music is like the sun in the sky
The harmony heard
The therapeutic sounds
The imagination of the songs scene
Music is like the sun in the sky
Singing in the car
Makes me feel like a star
The high pitch belting
Makes me want to start melting
Music is like the sun in the sky

— Sara R.
6th Grade

Lighthouse

The lighthouse lit the loomy water,
To show the boats the big bright boulders,
The dolphins dove into the dark,
Until the lighthouse lit the lake
The boat was dark and doomed
Until the lighthouse brightened the boulders.
The lighthouse it the loomy night
And made the boulders very bright

— Nora R.
6th Grade

My Music

Music makes my soul sing loud,
And makes me feel so very proud,
Music makes me forget my fumes of fury,
It makes me forget I'm in a hurry,
I feel so calm when I listen to my tune,
Makes me want to watch a cartoon.

— Nora R.
6th Grade

The Sky

Big, blue,beautiful,
the blue birds glide by
as the blue planes passes by
the big, boisterous, booming sound
filled the kids with blasphemy
watching this from the beautiful
translucent, blue waters on
a big boat in the Bahamas.

— Jocie M.
6th Grade

The Radio

When I turn on the radio
it's the new version of the stereo
I close my eyes and listen to
the booming beat. I roll down the
windows and feel the fresh air though
my hair. The roaming relaxation goes through
my horrible headache. The radio is almost
like a friend and their voice never
ends. Always there for me when the
sunrises to the sunsets, the saddest moments
to the biggest smile when I'm with my friends ...

— Jocie M.
6th Grade

You Are a Packaged Deal

The way you make me feel,
You make me want to get up and start dancing,
You are a packaged deal.
I feel okay when I hear your voice.
The way you make me think,
This is the thoughtful and thankful way to get the sad-
ness out from me.
Your voice helps me in ways no one can,
You are a packaged deal.

— Addison C.
6th Grade

Alliteration Poem

The cunning, careful girl
With characteristics of a cobra,
Is actually sweet, sympathetic, and smart,
Yet also beautiful, bodacious and blissful,
But feeling weary and worried for the world.
She thought, tried, and took her time,
Then voraciously voiced her thoughts,
Till the thoughts triumphed in other's minds.

— Sophia E.
6th Grade

Music Poem

The beat goes from
the cushioned headphones to my ears,
Then goes down to my happy, healthy heart.
The beat is so vibrant and clear,
Just listening diminished any of my fear.
When the song ends I again press start,
Then the more meaningful melodies of pop musics flow
through my happy, healthy heart.

— Sophia E.
6th Grade

EAST COOPER MONTESSORI SCHOOL

TEACHERS: **ANGIE ALVES AND NIKKI HOLLANDER**
POET INSTRUCTOR: **MARCUS AMAKER**
6TH – 7TH GRADE

People see a disorder,
I see a seed to sprout,
    Into something more,
Inside of me.

  A face of white skin,
And a mind that cannot find,
A constant state,
 A stare,
    A stain on me,
For all to see.

  Her aching arms struggle,
To push,
  The fearing bolder,
    Of getting older,
Off the edge,
From under the bed.

  To paint the perfect picture,
With the perfect pallet,
     With the perfect proportions.

  Her brown eyes,
Struggling to come,
 Face to face,
   With a place,
  Where she is tough,
Where she is enough.

A dark room,
   A dark wall,
  And a door,
That has yet to be opened.

 — Gwennyth S.
6th Grade

Distraught NO More

I am distraught.
I wonder if I'll ever be free from these chains of anxiety.
I hear a voice, calling, beckoning me out of darkness.
I am distraught.

I pretend to be okay.
Will the pain ever go away?
I hope one day, just like darkness fades,
This pain will fade and the light will shine.

I feel the chains of anxiety slipping away.
I cry, for I am free.
I thank my family for all that they've done for me.
From this day forward I will hold on with all my might,
Thank you, mom.
I love you.

— Kristine A.
7th Grade

We're killed by society
with words from your tongue
I don't get a say in things
because I am " young."

America doesn't see us as people
we are more like a target
we might as well get sold
on the black market.

I can't leave my home
without being scared
that the wrong cop
will see my "weapon"
and shoot me then and there.

I have a family.
Don't take me from them.
Don't make me feel unwanted.

You want me condemned,
I want a big major
and fulfill all my dreams
But you want me gone
as so it seems

But let me live.
I'll make my immigrant mother proud.

I'll walk across that stage
and get cheers from the crowd.

I'm in alien in your country.
But in mine, you're just a tourist.

We're the ones picking off of the plum trees
And people think America is the purist
My brown pigment is a part of me
I'm not ashamed of it
I am proud of it.

So just leave us alone
leave us be we
will not leave
we're here to commit.

So don't think you've won this fight, not yet.
We will stay here
because America isn't yours,
that's a bet.

I'll make it big in this world, you'll see
that's on sight
one day I'll get big
and earn all my right.

We are people, too.
We're not dangerous.
We only want to live, to be successful,
and have children.

We are all here with the same purpose
So don't scare my future children
don't make them forbidden

you say that "you're here for us"
but remember you voted to build that wall
You want to see us in cuffs
But you love our food
from what I recall

So think twice about what you will say
For when the times comes
I'll be ready for that day
I'm an alien in your country,
but in mine, you're welcomed .

— Carolina V.
6th Grade

JAMES ISLAND CHARTER HIGH SCHOOL

TEACHERS: NOLAN DAVIS AND REGINA COX-WASHINGTON
POET INSTRUCTOR: CHELSEA GRINSTEAD
9TH GRADE

Colors are dynamic,
they fall into the sky,
feels like it is winter.

— Anonymous
9th Grade

DARK
WAR

They sit in the silence while
at war

People stand to the see the
scars but laugh and ignore

Some win and some lose
but a cost is
deadly.

But some live to share
their story

— Drevan P.
9th Grade

Sad Meatball Hours

When meatball is sad
he goes into his room
to think about the past
No tears, no movement

His only company being
his thoughts his LED's
and sometimes his cat
He thinks until he can't

As he ruminates
he listens to the wind
on the outside of his window
The house shifts, and the wind wisps

His thoughts become a sinkhole
There's always a ladder waiting

He can leave when he wants.
I am Meatball

– Kenny R.
9th Grade

When I am sad I like to live in my
bed and listen to music to get what
happened out of my head. When I'm in
sad place there's tears but I wipe
them away. Break ups, switch ups,
mix ups and mess ups are what make me
upset

– De'Anna M.
9th Grade

93

music is like the ocean
and the lyrics flow like the waves
in a specific pattern they flow
and the person listening is like a man in a boat
calm and relaxed at peace

– Matthew H.
9th Grade

Colors are vibrant
through the sky clouds shine in the sky
feels like I'm mind blown

When I listen to music my head nods
With pleasure, music I treasure

I'm just here physically, mentally
I'm far far away
clouds fulfill my mind, the gentle
breeze rushing past my face

I believe in karma & that some people
are bound to get what's coming for them
beware of what you say or do to people

– Jaden C.
9th Grade

Colors are vibrant
clouds are floating in the sky
feels like things are going down hill.

– Skyy A.
9th Grade

LAING MIDDLE SCHOOL

TEACHERS: **MR. MOLINO AND GINA SCOTT**
POET INSTRUCTOR: **MARCUS AMAKER**
6TH GRADE

When You See Me

Claire
D

When you see me you say
There's the girl in the wheelchair
who reads all day

When you see me you say
yeah that girl
She's a loner
she barely has any friends

You don't see the girl
at home on crutches
just trying to relearn to walk

You don't see the girl
just laughing and talking
with her small group of friends

You don't see the girl
who only reads to escape from herself

You don't see the girl
just trying not to break down
when the world starts to frown

The girl that wishes
she could just be herself

The girl that's a
writer, a reader, a singer
yeah you don't see that girl
but that's who I truly am

When you look at me you see, blonde, braces, bold, tall and funny.
But when I look at myself I see anxiety and imperfections.
I am outgoing and messy, with a flowing stream of loyalty.
When my parents fight, I no longer see any light.
On the other side, I fly with my friends with integrity and freedom, in my little world, or magic kingdom.

-Amy L

Weird

Parker E

When people think weird,
they think something bad
When I think weird,
I think something unique
I am unique,
I am a super special someone
That is shining like the sun
Shining so bright that the world can see me
I am weird
And I like the way I am

My Spotlight

By June G

I see a bright light
I see crowds staring

They see a girl
Standing under that spotlight
Knees shaking unsteadily

A girl without grace,
Nor grit
Smooth emotions
I am not complicated
White, instead of the shade of brown I really am

This is how they see but
I feel the stage under my feet
My voice raised readily
To relearn myself from the words my soul poured out

They don't see my complexities
But they hear my voice

My voice is who I am to them
For that is what they hear

But what I see
Is myself

Me

When people look at me
It is a young boy that they see
When I look at me
Mad and sad
A man I see
Proud and smart
Brave and strong
I am a high hill
Yet a mound, scared and weak
Is what those who know me see

But I worry not
For what I see
Is a boy
Cool, curious, and creative
And my belief is all that I need

- Wren A

A Butterfly Garden

Kathryn S

A beautiful garden,
Filled with beautiful butterflies,
A spirit flies when a soul dies,
Never to be seen again,
Nothing for me to gain.

When you look at me you may see a
self doubtful little girl but if you look
on the inside you see sassy, smart, strong, and a
selfless women. She could be talented, brave, and a leader
But if you don't search for it you'll never find it.
I know that the ones who truely love me see what i see
Some people get butterflies when they look into my green
eyes
All they can see is the true me

    -Lucy J

This is me...

This is me... Beyond
Beautiful Brave Bold
Brown not Black love
my skin i rather be a
cat not a rat... I love
my skin it's a nice brown
color, love my hair it's natural
and Im not afraid
to show it... I wrote this
to a poet so I could
show it...

This is me!

and i hope
you know it♥

BY : Amary
K
4/6/22

103

When you look at me you see
that I am smart
but when I look at myself,
I think that I can be a work of art
I see something different
I am not very snarky
All my friends see me and smile
but others,
they see me away from a mile
I'm a cool calm collected kid
but others see me as an crazy bid!
But the mirror doesn't lie
no one can tell who I am on the inside!

Effie ♥

When you look at me you see...
a young girl who wears glasses
and look kinda silly, but when I look
at myself i know i might be those, but
im more, I'm a girl who loves violin
and her friends i might overthink
sometimes but it doesn't stop me
from being as outgoing as possible

Brianna

When you look at me,
you see that I'm athletic,
rich, rough, a young man and a busman,
But I'm really a stiff, has some money, carful,
a real fan and a little boy.

Like, when you look at the rock they think a tough guy.
But he really is a soft family guy that does Disney movies
When you look at a jaw breaker on the outside it is hard like a rock.
But when you crack the jaw breaker open it is soft like a bunny.

— Jake C.

"KNOW ME"

A Lot of people know me as a quiet girl but you really won't know me unless you look inside my world. I LOVE fashion designing, and i'm really sensitive but not everyone knows i'm also very stylish. So don't think you know me if you didn't look but to be honest you're probably a vicious crook.

- Janiyah M.

Poem: How I wish the world would be

The world is crazy and rapidly changing,
people in Ukraine are scared and shakeing.
Chaos around the world turning to fighting and war,
people don't know whats true on TV anymore.

Propagandas all over no one knows what to do,
who to trust or who to listen to.
Fighting and conflict, covid and disease,
when will this end? When will this conflict be eased?

when will the world open their eyes and see,
how the world really could be?
Focuse on the good and not the bad,
remember what Love is and stop makeing
People feel so Sad.

Help people up, don't bring them down,
Show them how their welcome In your town.
Treat people fairly, not like animals or beasts,
but treat them like people, because were all equal.

— Elise 10

MOULTRIE MIDDLE SCHOOL

TEACHER: **JULIA KUEHN**
POET INSTRUCTOR: **MARCUS AMAKER**
7TH GRADE

T'was I Enough?

Why would you compare?
For was I, not enough?
Not enough for whom?
For I was perfect for myself.

A dark storm cloud
That ruins young -
Young who are no longer happy.

For you destroyed them
Like a predator
Crushing its prey

Like the unmannerly,
Uncivil, vast predator you are
For the reminisce
That clouds over me
Whilst I'm confident
I suddenly wilt,
Like a dead rose,
Abandoned and over.

— Catherine C.
7th Grade

My Comfort Spot

He was my comfort spot
My comfort spot whilst I lay distraught
The sound of his voice, pure joy
Pure joy he brought
He was truly a comfort spot

With my uncle, dreams arised
The phone call every night
The characters I would hear
Driving me straight into a deep sleep
Knowing, I had a comfort spot
A comfort spot for this little dot

— Catherine C.
7th Grade

Life

In November,
I was hurt,
humbled and hardened.
My life crumbled
in front of me
and my life
fumbled.

In January,
I was scared,
sorry, and sad.
Eventually, I learned
My dad was the only thing
that didn't make me
sad.

In February,
I learned,
listened, and loved.
I learned to accept me
and see that I am
who I am.

In March,
I was happy,
humble, and honest.
I felt like God saved me
and gave me a
second chance.

— Emily G.
7th Grade

Unnamed

The world looks at me
and they see a nerdy know-it-all with glasses and books.
The world looks at me
but doesn't see a kid who likes running
and has a good memory.
A kid who isn't afraid to say what is on his mind.
Someone not afraid to fight for what is right.
Someone who helps those around him.
This is what the world is blind to.

— Jamison K.
7th Grade

Average

I appear tall, nice and average.
Messy hair. Disorganized.
But that is a mask
hiding my real traits.

Streaks of artistic background run through my veins
Guitar riffs rock in my head.
Tie fighters zip around my ADHD
filled my memories of fun times with friends.

Family shouting
Babies pouting cause Mom
won't buy them Fortnite skins.

This is my life of jumbled photos and opportunity.
I'm a jack of all trades
Ups and downs and false truths
My life isn't perfect
I'm full of thoughts that confuse people
Fitting in is something I used to try
Now I don't feel like living a lie.

This is what people see or don't
but it's for all to know.

— William V.
7th Grade

Life

When you look at me, you see a shy person
One who is quiet

When I look at myself, I see someone different
Energetic and strong

Always active
Amazingly awesome

Silly and self-aware
Straight forward

Willing to play ball
Tall

So when you look
you see a shy person who is quiet.

I see me.

— Nathaniel G.
7th Grade

When I Walk In

When I walk in they see me
but they don't *see* me
They see a quiet
shy, kind, ginger
but what they don't see
is the confident, loud
fun, loyal side of me

When I walk in they think,
oh well -
she doesn't talk.

They don't see the
big booming blossom
that is me.

When I walk in they
see what I pretend to be
to cover up
the person that is me.

— Emma P.
7th Grade

Portrait Poem

When you see me, you see a basic brown haired girl
Who has simple freckles
And always chuckles
When I look at myself
I see a young youthful girl
Who is sensitive
Who has few frivolous flaws
And has a heart for animals
But once you get to know me,
I can be caring as can be
I do have anxiety
And hopes for everything to be perfect
But I am me.

— Emerson D.
7th Grade

She is Her

She is her
They see smiles,
They see grades,
They don't see the fright,
They don't the optimism,
to a fault,
They don't see the reasons,
Her mind is offset,
Her skills are mixed,
Her voice is loud,
Her music is quiet,
She knows what her life is,
But never what she is,

Change is normal,
Stability hurts,
She's bubbling breaking,
Never screaming out just sorting in,
Her thoughts get filed,
Her feelings trapped,
In a sea of normal,
She pops out like a stain,
She doesn't understand you,
She can't,
I am her

— Holiday G.
7th Grade

When I look in a mirror
I see tall girl, short hair
I hear my loud voice and
my casual style is there

But what mirrors can't reflect
are my anxious thoughts
or my dramatic reactions
I wish they would stop

But it also can't show
the things that I like
I love science class
Be a doctor? I might

Mirrors can't reflect
My joyful, jumpy spirit
No the mirror can't see,
reflect, or hear it

Mirrors can't show
the things I believe
my religion and culture
are things it can't see

Mirrors can't show what
I think or believe
but I can show everything;
I can show me.

— Fin B.
7th Grade

Medium height wears a watch
As you can see
Nothing that special about me
Academic and artful, but I still worry
My doubts around me in a flurry

But if you look deep down
past the fretful fear
you will see I keep
all my identity near.
From kind to funny
unique and mindful
on time, never late

That is my fate
I love to code
Dogs are my passion
Not full of fashion
This is me
What you don't see

— Maximilian C.
7th Grade

When you look at me you see a short boy
but when I look at myself, I see something different.
I see a creative, intelligent, person who tries his best

I am creative, intelligent, and also love to rest.
But when you see me, you think I am super short and
stubby.
But the mirror doesn't lie,
I am awesome, amazing, and face things head-on,
ablazing.

— Carter S.
7th Grade

When you look at me,
you see nothing abnormal just a sports player,
my sport is very special to me
but for some, it is hard to see

My sport will make you bashed and bruised
ruthless and rumbled but
you will end up accomplished and amazed,
now that's why my sport is no longer only special to me
but my entire community

— Stone C.
7th Grade

When you see me
You see a young teenage girl
You see a girl who wears a mask
Some athlete
Maybe you see the black girl you can't be racist around
Maybe you think I'm ugly
Maybe you think I'm pretty
Some may not see or think any of this
But that's how I feel you see me
Especially at school
At school, I hear people say the "N" word and not care
At school, I hear people say other offensive things
School sees me without my personality
What the world doesn't see
A girl who feels like the ugly duckling
A girl who can be really funny
Nobody sees how much I play Roblox
The world doesn't see how my mental health declined
The world doesn't see how sensitive I can be to words
The world doesn't see who I am or what I deal with
The world will never see 100% me.

— Anonymous
7th Grade

I'd like to think I'm getting better,
No longer bundled up in that cold sweater
Finally feeling that warmth,
That happiness
That many told me, was deserved
Has that happiness just been,
Preserved?
The entire time?

— Catherine C.
7th Grade

Who I am

They see me as a
Shy, sweet, smart, unique
13 year old blonde haired girl
but thats not all
of what I am
I have severe OCD + ADHD
but thats not all
I have Dyslexia
thats what makes me stick out
but thats not all
I am fast, flexable, and furious
I do competitive gymnastics, dance, and pointe
And thats what makes me
Who I am

— Madelyn S

Kennedy P

Other people see that
i am a tall young girl
with dark frizzy hair
but a lot of the time i dont care
how i look is not my fortake
but what people think makes my heart race
Im anxious about anonymous things
and jagged jacked janky teeth with wires that
pull them together
but pokey powerful springs to fix it
Im kind an caring and enjoy honesty
and my strong brain wipes out tests like
a freight train
now other people see
what makes up me

123

Emma K

maybe you'll see on the feild
maybe in class
but not through the glass
You can see my blonde straight hair
do you see me straightening it in the mirror
I worry about what the world sees
But then I remember they don't know me
They don't know my loud, leader personality
or my strong, silly, sweet self
maybe if they look in my mirror
could they see the real me?

When you look at me,
you see a tall,
weird, annoying girl
but there's more to me
then what meets the eye.
I see something different,
I see a smart, funny,
freindly little girl
who just wants to
be liked.
I see a calm person
with a big imagination,
who doesn't know how to act.
I see the worst in myself.
I wonder,
is that what everyone
else sees?

Virginia D.

When the world looks at me it sees
a tall, outgoing, athlete
But the world doesn't stop to see the deeper
inside
They only glance to see the rightside
not the wrong
When I look at me, I see the inside
The madness, that goes on in my mental
magnificient mind.
internaly filled with anger, and anxiety
when the world sees the portrait of me
they think
an athlete with no problems
but yes
inside my head is thoughts of failure
and when I do fail
I am left with anger
But no one seems to see
because I put up a friendly face, not
showing the fierce problems.

Skye D

Even though I am usually seen as
bubbly, boisterous and bright,
I know that I struggle with
anxiety.

Even though I am usually seen as
smiley and happy
all of the time,
I know that I have been shaped
by my past expirences.

Even though I am usually seen as
crazy and loud,
I am a great person to
just sit and talk to for hours

I always seem to put others before
myself every single time,
but what do I do when
Its just myself every single time.

—— Wren K

When you look at me, you see
a thirteen year old girl,
an honor roll student
a happy, care free pearl
a perfectly, prostegious procrastinator
When I look at me, I see
Someone who is always stressing out
a person pretending to the world
Someone who has major trust issues
Someone who always has sadness within
I want you to see
the outside does not show what's in the inside
the world is quick to judge
to not truly see what's inside

—Emily R.

average by reagan

"average."
like I ever heard that one before
hated by the school
though I try hard to be "cool"
Try walking up in my shoes
"you're an emo"
is what I'm titled as
though I may be tall,
that is not all
I'm funny when you get to know me
and all I laugh at is monke
an average kid I am?
I can draw
and I have an amazing channel :>
I am not actually annoying
What you see isn't me

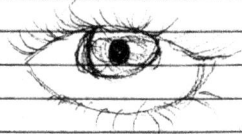

reagan j

When you see me,
You want to make stereotypes.
Small, Quiet, and a girl with glasses.
Those things may be true,
But take a look inside.
You now see a creative girl,
maybe a smart girl,
I am energetic and musical.
All of these things are true.
When you see me now,
You will know the truth.

— Jillian L

Poem

When you look at me you see a girl whos happy and smart but when I look at myself I see something different, I see a girl with bad skin, gross braces, and annoys everyone around me. When you look at me you see the same boring, bland, and basic shoes but I see my only Christmas gift from my step dad. When you talk to me you hear a girl who seems calm but really I don't want to annoy you with my unpleasing, uninteresing, and undesirable voice. I can't go a day without cleaning because If I do ill never get around to it. I can't sleep one night witout a stuffed annual my dad gave me because if I do I worry I'll forget him. When you look at me you choose to see what isnt worrying but if you really get to see the honest, and caring me, you may be suprised by what you see but this is the true me.

— Erin E

131

Life is a roller coaster.
It is a cycle.
You go up
and go down.
You may laugh.
"Ha! Ha!"
You may scream.
"AAAH!"
You may cry
"Waaah!"
But you will get over it.
and want to do it again!

"Life is a Roller Coaster"   By: Jillian L

NORTH CHARLESTON CREATIVE ARTS ELEMENTARY

TEACHER: **MR. VISSER**
POET INSTRUCTOR: **MARJORY WENTWORTH**
4TH AND 5TH GRADE

The Morning

I wake up to my mother yelling my name
to get up. I brush my teeth and the minty smell burns
my eyes.

I go wake up my little brother
shaking him five times
and he starts to whine.

I walk downstairs and stub my toe,
Ow! The burning never stops.
I grab our clothes and go upstairs.
We finally put on our clothes.

I put on my favorite hoodie
it is so warm, I grab my Chromebook
but hesitate and I shove it in my bookbag.

We go downstairs, I grab
a cold drink.
It's colder than our freezer
and then we walk
to the bus stop.

— Carielle G.
5th Grade

Morning Rain

As I awake I smell my mom making
fresh morning coffee.
I hear the coffee grounds
crunching and crackling.

I put my pile of stuffed animals beside me.
As I yawn and stretch
I hear the raindrops.
They sound like acorns dropping.

I get out of my bunk bed
and take all my stuffed animals
and reorganize them.
I go say good morning to my siblings
and my mom, then I let my dogs out.
They push me out of the way
and they run like cheetahs.

My mom and I will go make breakfast.
I step on the cold icy floor
and run to get my slippers,
then we make breakfast together.

— Anja T.
5th Grade

Morning

I wake up in the morning
and made some coffee;
smells like Heaven.
Hear a ding!
Oh no, Dad's awake.
Ow!
Coffees too hot.

Remember to charge my watch
Starts at 61%
Ends at 89%
Put it on my wrist and say,
"Mom, wake up!"

Change my clothes
and make my bed.
Bread dipped in coffee
tastes like cheesecake,
a bit better though.

Enter my car
but it's cold like an iceberg.
I ask my dad for the keys.
Phew, it's warming up.
Well, I'm off to school.

— Jackson S.
5th Grade

My Morning

5:30 I wash my face
and iron my clothes
Watch the steam rise.

I greet my dad
with a half-awake
hello,
as he responds
with a smile.

Put on my warm clothes
along with my shoes
as I enjoy the smell of coffee
and the morning news.

I walk out the door,
get in the car
and listen
to the sad-like Blues.

— Shavon R.
5th Grade

School Day

When you first wake up, notice
the covers are always
pulled from you.

Going to brush
your teeth
as fast
as the speed of light.

A thin layer
of frost
on the window.

Tasting the mint toothpaste
you hurry and put
your shoes
and jacket on.

Not able to smell
the fresh coffee
or warm cornbread,
you lay on your bed.
It's warm.
Did you forget something?

— Melisa R.
5th Grade

Butter Biscuits

As I wake up I smell hot butter biscuits.
I hear my mom and dad
calling me. I see my mom
coming into my room.

I go to the kitchen
in my pajamas;
sleepy
and
tired.

The sweet buttery biscuits
taste like warm pancakes
melting in my mouth.

I eat my biscuits and think
to myself. Asking my mom
if I can make some
for the neighbor.
My mom
says yes.

— Gabriella M.
5th Grade

Morning

Ding, ding, ding, click!
I roll out of bed
dragging my feet.
I turn on the light
as my eyes open as bright
as the sun.

Yawn.
I drag myself
to the bathroom hearing
the birds chirp. I grab
the minty toothpaste
and brush my smelly teeth.

I hear a loud voice call,
"Hurry up!"
I march to the car
feeling the cold icy weather.
I eat buttery pancakes
and an orange.

I march to class hearing
all the noise behind me.
It sounds like a party.

— Ja'Niyah H.
5th Grade

My Morning

Lick, lick, lick! The feeling of my dog
licking me makes me feel excited.
The sight of cold water
sends shivers down my spine.

The mouth watering pancakes
are as soft as cotton.
The sound of birds chirping
makes everything peaceful.

The sound of the car radio
bores me, so I turn
it off.

The
train
stops.
Everyone
waits.

The ride was as long as a giraffe's neck,
but at least this is the end.

— Hilary M.
5th Grade

Morning Poem

When I wake up in the morning
I'm as cold as ice.
I go to brush my teeth
with toothpaste as minty
as a peppermint candy cane
on Christmas.

When I go downstairs
my breakfast is as hot as a volcano.
I tried to eat it and burnt my mouth
on the spoon, but the oatmeal
smelled so good, I couldn't resist.

I go and get ready for school,
put all my clothes on
and my new fluffy coat
that feels like clouds.

I go wait for the bus,
but I'm late! I run
as fast as a flash.
Finally I get on the bus
and make it in time for class.

— Zy'Mare S.
5th Grade

My Morning

I wake up at six
My alarm buzzes like flies
buzzing around me. I brush my teeth
the mint burns my mouth
like hot sauce.

I brush my hair
half-asleep
like a zombie.
I get dressed, the clothes
so cold sitting on the hook
all night.

I put my school laptop
in my backpack
with my water bottle
and go to school.

In the car that smells like mint,
heading to school, my brother
and dad talk
a lot.
A LOT.
Thinking about my bed.

— Kate S.
4th Grade

Morning

When I first wake up
I moan and groan
and wait for mom
to come out of the shower.
While I wait
I go on TikTok.

When mom finally comes out, I grab
my plain black t-shirt
and head to the bathroom
to brush my teeth.

I come out and put on socks
and shoes and start the car. I sit
for five minutes, then mom comes out

I turn on the heater
to heat my seat. I'm sleepy
but excited and ready to learn!

— Paris L.
4th Grade

Waiting

When I first wake up
I hear my grandmother calling my name.
I feel the teal brush combing through my hair.
My toothbrush sounds like a bee buzzing.

I go downstairs to pack my lunch,
it smells so good I might take
a bite. I grab a breakfast bar.
Crunch,
crunch,
crunch.

In the car
my seatbelt clicks. I see
the clouds in the window.
I can almost see school.

Waiting,
waiting,
waiting.
I see the time.
Five
more
minutes.
More waiting.
Finally, it's time for school!

— Libby H.
4th Grade

Morning Wake-up

I wake up and hear my annoying alarm clock.
Walking down the stairs
I taste my bad breath.

I go downstairs to get my breakfast,
my dad sounds like nails on a chalk board
telling me to let the dog out.

When I do, I feel the cold breeze
shivering up my spine
like a ghost walking through me.

I smell my mom's morning coffee,
and taste my morning breakfast.
My toothpaste tastes
like fresh mint.

I put my shoes on
and head out with my heavy backpack.
I hear myself mumbling as quiet as a mouse
saying, "I want to go back to sleep."

— Laney T.
5th Grade

Time to Go

"Wake up!" I hear my parents yell.
I get up and smell my breath,
it's as stinky as a smelly sock.
I take a shower
as warm as a hot summer day.

I taste the minty toothpaste
on my tongue. My mom yells,
"You're going to be late!"
I grab my sock and shoes
and put them on.

I brush my hair
feeling the tangled pieces
from taking a shower.

I get into the warm car
and we get to school -
On time!

— Ava U.
5th Grade

Wakeup

Click! The light turns on as fast as a blink.
GET UP! My eyes drop as I try to stand.
The cold touch of the floor is like snow.

My legs feel numb, the hot water crashing
down feels like bee stings. The cool crisp air
flows through my body.

The soft warm cloth feels like a hairy
dog. My sock touch the floor like a warrior
protecting my feet.

The icy breeze flashes through me as I open
the door. My body freezes like a rock when I
touch the cold metal handle.

— Kilani L.
5th Grade

Mondays

When I wake up
I roll out of bed
and get dressed half-asleep.
I brush my hair and teeth,
I see the blurry image of a door.

I tip-toe downstairs
to fill my water bottle.
As my eyes focus on the kitchen
I hear the light click of a door.

I go to put my shoes on
and stumble out the door.
Greeted by frigid air
that sends a chill down my spine.

I collapse into the seat of our car
and fall asleep as the car rumbles
while the NPR host speaks
with a quiet whisper whisking me asleep.

— Vivian H.
5th Grade

When I Wake Up

When I first wake up,
my dad cuts the lights on.
It's as bright as the sun. I walk
into the shower and feel the hot water
on my skin.

I hear my mother calling me
to breakfast; her voice as sweet
as a dove. As I bite into a hot pocket
I taste the cheesy goodness.
After eating, I feed Zeus.

As we walk outside
to the bus stop, I feel the cold air
touch my skin. It's as cold as ice.

As I walk onto the bus
I say one final "Goodbye"
to my dad.

— Ruby H.
5th Grade

Morning Time

I wake up still half asleep,
get out of bed and get dressed.
I smell the fresh bacon
sizzling in the pan. I hear my mom
yell my nickname, "AJ, come to the table!"

I run into the bathroom
and brush my teeth. I get to the kitchen
and see the bacon and pancakes sitting
on the table.

I go check on my brother
who is crying as loud as a fire engine siren.
Once I calm him
I go to the table and start eating.

When I'm finished I go outside
and sit
in the cold car
and wait
for my brother and granddad.

— Antonio G.
5th Grade

My Morning Poem

When I wake up in the morning
I see that my alarm turned off
by itself when I was asleep.

When I get up and go to the bathroom
I hear my dogs barking
and my mom is brewing coffee.
It sounds like rain dripping
from the sky.

When I walk back into my room
I smell perfume in the air
and the strong smell of coffee.

I feel the cold air rush against my skin
when I walk past the air vent.
I go to the kitchen
and eat some breakfast
with my mom.

— Kamari B.
5th Grade

Morning Routine

At six o'clock my dad turns on the light.
I can see it through my eyelids,
but I just can't wake up,
so my dad tickles my feet.
I feel his cold smooth hands
touch my warm feet.

When I finally get out of bed
I put my socks on.
They feel as warm as the sun.
I go downstairs still half-asleep.

I put on my backpack
that feels like the weight of an elephant,
and I put on my coat.
After I take the trash out
that smells like a skunk,
I start the car.

When I start the car
I feel the engine rumbling -
It sounds like a lion roaring.
I turn the heat up all the way to high
and the heated seats
for my brother and mom.

— Blake R.
5th Grade

PALMETTO SCHOLARS ACADEMY

TEACHERS: **BETSY MILLER AND JUNIUS WRIGHT**
POET INSTRUCTOR: **EVELYN BERRY**
9TH – 11TH GRADE

Arthur Avenue

Kalief Browder, held without trial on Rikers Island in solitary confinement for three years, committed suicide in 2015.

in that moment
on arthur avenue,
my life was thieved from me.
but back then,
i was the thief.
those three years at rikers killed me.
all alone i was in that cell.
the screeching silence,
the cold cement walls clawing at my dark skin.
i still remember
those orange jumpsuits.
the ones that smelt of
aggressive, selfish, animalistic, greedy
and most importantly, guilty
criminals.
except, they weren't criminals.
more like monsters.
those orange jumpsuits
mocked me. they called me all sorts
of names. they said i was just like them.
i'm not one of them,
i'm not a monster.
sometimes i think back
way back to that time
on arthur avenue.
and those sometimes i wonder
what my life would have been like
if i could just go home.

— Kharisma B.
10th Grade

Heaven Alight

Notre dame is burning down
The fire bright as angels descending from the heavens
As heaven fades the structure crumbles
The angels descend, carried by wings of flame
The soul of god are among Notre Dame's ashes

— Sebastian H.
9th Grade

Big Bangn't

Only to return when men have fallen
the one true god sneaks into their ranks.
Impersonating the youngins,
in a body made of flesh,
the one true god falters as
it immerses itself.
Never,
ever,
in existence,
has it failed,
so spectacularly.
Purple,
orange,
colors that can't be explained.
Swirls,
curls,
infinite dendrograms
Physics,
mathematics,
theoretical sciences,
all out the nonexistent window.
It never would have been thought,

and never will be thought
that
the only true god would have failed
so extravagantly.

— Sebastian H.
9th Grade

The Boy & The Box

There once was a boy with a box
His box was too small
He could not fit at all
He was as big as an ox
He went to town
Asked one and all
For a bigger box
For his was too small
Everyone said the box was his
So he should be able to fit his all
He showed the town
That his body sticked out
And he couldn't fit at all
They laughed and yelled
Said that he smelled
And their words hurt like rocks
The boy got rid of the box
The boy left town
Went to the woods
And stumbled upon a fox
He asked the fox
"Why no box?"
The fox was confused

His curiosity pursued
And he answered with
"Why box?"
The boy understood
He did as he should
He made himself a box
It was big and all
It was no longer too small
The boy and the box

— Eriq B.
10th Grade

That Funny Feeling

Love is kind of an abstract thing.
But gay love?
What a terrifying and lovely feeling.
We fought for our right to love who we want to love.
Even put in death camps just because the difference
scares others.
The 1930's were a terrifying time.
Pink triangles on our chests are outing us to the world.
Somehow I believe we will get to be ourselves some day.

— Scarlett H.
11th Grade

Destruction Against Two Gods

Towns being Torched left and right
Dead people all around in the blamed villages
Different people who see different Gods
This all happened in a series of nights
Police got involved day one,
Tensions were high
Two days later Muslims beating Hindus
Even the Temples though it was not done
2 Hindus were killed on that day
Torching the Temples they did
No Police or Ambulances came to help
it was joy for us, but to them was grey
On the other side it was all the same
They hated us, we hated them
It was not that we were Indian or Bengali
No, it was the religion to blame
Keeping this up, hate will not go down
We both have feelings and are people
We see the same sunlight and sunset
Our mothers gave us the same skin, we are Brown

— Afif U.
10th Grade

SANDERS-CLYDE CREATIVE ARTS ELEMENTARY SCHOOL

TEACHERS: MS. HEYWARD, MS. KNIGHT, MS. TAYLOR, MS. STRAIGHT, MS. SIMS, MS. WRAY, MS. DALY, MS. HONAKER, MS. FREE, MS. MCGEE, MS. WELLS, MS. BROOKS
POET INSTRUCTOR: MARCUS AMAKER
3RD AND 4TH GRADE

Pretty Puma's Wedding

Purly is planting pretty
purple flowers and
painting playful
pictures. Purly is collecting
pretty pearls for a
pretty wedding party.
There are paintings and
pretty flowers for
the pretty wedding
for pretty Puma
who is waiting, waiting,
for her pretty wedding
with her princely
pretty man.

— Yasmin R.
3rd Grade

Camilo

Camilo traveled to California
With his cat.
He was acting so cool,
But the hot car
made him sweat.
He opened the window
To catch a chill but instead
He got a cold.
The chilly breezy
Caused him to catch
A cold.

— Courtney J.
3rd Grade

The mom only makes magic
when it's a full moon.
She uses her magic for the
movement for major problems.

— Janell W.
4th Grade

Terrance

Terrance drank some
Tea then he went to
go play
with his toy train.
Then he raced
Ty'Rasha and they
had a tie.
Terrance and Ty'Rasha loved
The color teal. They made tiles.

— Terrance G.
3rd Grade

Boston

I thought I was a Boston butterfly
Building, riding a bug
Because the ride was
Too bouncy.
I was in Boston.

— Suede W.
3rd Grade

Gabby

Gabby grows green
In Georgia
To get great grapes.

— Gabrielle H.
3rd Grade

Ty'Raisha

Ty'Raisha turns ten tomorrow
But she felt terrible.
On a terrible Tuesday her mom told her
She will take them to Target so
She can feel better tomorrow.

— Ty'Raisha D.
3rd Grade

Beyonce
Boxes
Big
Brown
Blue
Black.

— Beyonce T.
3rd Grade

Sheep

Soft fluffy sheep sleep and
jump in fluffy softly clouds.
The sheep jumps and plays in
the fluffy, puffy, cotton clouds.
The sheep like hopping over the fence.
The sheep live in the
south of their silent farm.

— I'Laysia E.
4th Grade

Londyn

Londyn is a rich, rare,
and red rosy bunny.
Run on the race track.
Londyn lifts up a flag.
Londyn laughs with joy.

— Javaiha J.
4th Grade

Saturn

Saturn sits in the galaxy sadly in the solar system.
The sun shines on the galaxy
The solar system spins slowly around the shining sun.
The sun shines on the states.
The solar system reflects the sun's shine
and the sun shines on the stars.

— Kylah P.
4th Grade

My Apple

The apple I ate was so good then I ate a candy apple.
But the ants came and tried to eat it.
Then I ate another apple. But it was green.
Then this time the queen came and all the littles.
They took my apple and said they will pay me back.
They gave me candy and a green apple.
And then they gave me gold.

— Ayanna E.
4th Grade

The Snake

The slippery snake slithers back home. Slithers and
slides to the swamp and makes soup to eat. He went to
the market to get some carrots. He slithers and meets
the most prettiest snake in the world. She said hi and
so did he. They became best friends and slithered to
a snake restaurant. They had some mice and rats and
slithered happily to the swamp to play Snake.

— Tamaria J.
4th Grade

Breakfast

At breakfast we had sausage
and sweet sauce at the small table.
We all were sitting.
The sausage was so good with the sweet sauce
and the table was so sparkly.
I love breakfast in the morning at the small table.

— Carmen W.
4th Grade

Rainbow

After it rains, the rainbow rises
and the rich kid follows it till the end of it.
Then Richard raced the rich kid for the pot of gold.
And he won the pot of gold.
And Richard spent the riches on bills and a
round home for his relatives.
Richard ran into the hospital now
and he had the money to pay for it
His mother was fully healed
and she was put in a wheel chair
And he surprised her with a new home and new car.

— Alexandria G.
4th Grade

Basketball

I bounced the brown basketball
but the brown ball was flat.
So I blew it up so it could bounce
up and down
and not be flat again.

— Londyn G.
4th Grade

The Man

Can the man is a hero and the hero is the man.
The man is getting bands.
And the man can have the can
and the money to buy the can.
The man is happy because he is the hero.
The hero helped people so they can be safe.

— Emil W.
4th Grade

Raven

Raven ran the race track
And she
saw a rainbow.

— Celeste G.
4th Grade

My Poem

My mom used to tell me to master my inner self,
So I mimic Martin Luther King Jr.
She used to say it was mandatory to unlock my
mysterious character.
So now I'm ready to give
my maximum. I am myself.
I am Behold.

— Behold S.
4th Grade

The Baby

The baby babbled because
he wanted his bottle
and he bopped his head on the bottle.

— Takai G.
4th Grade

Roger

Roger, the rich boy
Ran to the race track
With a red flag.
He hates running in the rain,
but wanted to race.
After he raced,
Roger wished he was at Red Robin.

— Jamier W.
4th Grade

The Door

"Hey door," said Divine.
"Darn it, what do you want," said the door.
"What is behind you?
Is it dark and dreary, or is it brighter than the sun?"
The door opened itself.
It was dark.
Divine dared herself to go down.
"Wow, sure is dark down there."

— Divine T.
5th Grade

Marcus

In March, Marcus went to a museum.
He used a map to get there.
On the way he drank some maple juice.
When he was finished he listened to some music.
On the way home he got lost again, so he used a map.

— Zion J.
5th Grade

Mysterious Mist

A mysterious mist became more and more misty.
The misty meadows air was a danger to the mist.
Where the mist had met the meadow's mist,
there was a Museum of Mouse.
The mouse of the museum
marched through the mist and got lost.
Then by the guide of a map,
they managed to make a way
to the meadow with the most air.

— Unknown
5th Grade

EUGENE SIRES ELEMENTARY SCHOOL

TEACHER: **SUZANNE MILLER**
POET INSTRUCTOR: **WILL DAVIS**
4TH GRADE

Name Madelyn

Autumn over drive

I wonder at the taste and the smells that fill my home, and that brings nutriton to my body and warth to my bones.

Thank you lord for the reason and understanding that we ofen take for granted, thank you for the mystery of life and the perfet way you planned it

Thank you lord for the abundance at my table, and for the breath of my lungs and the limbs that make able

On thanks giving I think of the crisp autum breeze and the the jingle of the keys.

I am thankfull for all, because some kan't even call

My family comes on the same day ech year and the message is clear

I am thank full for the food at my table because some are not able.

thanksgiving

The year has turned it's circle
The seasons come and go
The harvest all is gatheredin
And chilly north winds blow
Orchards have shared their treasures
The fields their yellow grain
So open wide the doorway
Thanksgiving comes again

Gobble, gobble, gobble
It's time to do a trot
Let's eat cooked broc
And find thanksgiving rocks
It's time to rock the baby
And get crazy

Thanksgiving with family is the best

Name Tristin

A Thanksgiving Blessing

It's cold outside, but it's warm in my heart,
And the gray fall sky is His work of art. Laden and
low, quiet and still, November is welcome, and my eyes
drink their fill.

Of brown-gray grass and red-orange leaves, of pavemen[t]
winding through the strong, stately trees. Down
the hill, past the barn, past the gate, up the lane.
The house with bright candels in the window pain.
Now I step inside: Oh, it's warm! Oh, that smell!
Hot turkey roasting, potatoes done well! Sweet, spicy
cider, and warm winter wind. Cranberry sauce - oh!
The flavors are divine!

The smiles and hugs are so warm and sweet. In this
cold gray November, a Thanksgiving treat. I do love
it all and am so thankful; yes, for this lovely season
I am truly blessed.

Name Damian

Thanksgiving

Thanksgiving is memorable.

Thanksgiving is full of hope.

Thanksgiving is nostalgic.

It feels like a rope.

Thanksgiving goes by fast,

While being very vast.

Everyone is talking about the past.

Thanksgiving is essential.

Thanksgiving is rejoiced.

You hear every voice.

We are all there to see.

What the world will come to be.

In the family's greatest dreams.

Name Lilly

Thanksgiving is here!
when the leaves fall
and
when you smell cinnamon

Thanksgiving is
here!
when a chatter begins to spread
and
you can feel the heat
from the oven

Thanksgiving is
here!
when the feast is near
and
the blessing begins

Thanksgiving is

here!

Name _____

My thanksgiving poem

Thanksgiving is fun. Thanksgiving is great. Thanksgiving
is nice. Sometimes we have rice. My family and I cook
together. In my house. We always cook turky no
other meat. For our vegtables we have Green Bean
Cassoroll and sweetpotatos with marshmellows. Then we all
eat together. ♡ I love my family and they love me. Even
though not all of my family loves eachother, I love all of
them, and they all love me. love you guys! ♡

Name _Sidney # 7_

My Thanksgiving

Deer for dinner, instead of turky.
pumkin pie, if I get lucky.
football and games and fun times too.
Thinking of my grant paula, while watching the
faireunfilm.

Happy Thanksgiving
everyone!

Name Chloe

ThanksGiving. ThanksGiving.

ThanksGiving ThanksGiving food food turkey, stree throught, and Creole to. ThanksGiving Thanksgiving family Ada, Vann, Garon, Grany, Granny, Grandma, and don't forget Carry. ThanksGiving ThanksGiving tradition tradition ThanksGiving parade, turkey competion. ThanksGiving ThanksGiving When gets dark we all get quiet sit around and watch The Peanuts Movie. Shh! Shh! Now we are asleep. ThanksGiving.

WANDO HIGH SCHOOL

TEACHER: **LYNNE POGGIOLI**
POET INSTRUCTOR: **MARCUS AMAKER**
9TH – 12TH GRADE

Elephants and Donkeys: A Branded Babies Cry

We have Branded our Babies with the same irons that
once burned our own backs.
Swamps of Red and Blue stamps form a so-called
'United' States
veiled in a cloak of sovereignty, Integrity, and
Hypocrisy.
January 6th, 2021; the cloak fell.
The Branded Babies of Branded Babies witnessed a
nation fold at a seam of Red and Blue.
In the very place where questions resolved themselves
in peace, now haunted by five spirits.
Five spirits lost in a purple storm, cast over the nation.

We Brand our Babies for our own sake, to ensure they
aren't mistaken for another.
The practice of Branding the Babies of Branded Babies
is now tradition. Why wouldn't it be?
We have been preaching to a choir of like-branded
people since we forged the first iron in the fire of hope.
Our like-branded people are an unknown family, a
secret society with only the strictest dress code.

What happens when a Branded Baby cries?
What happens when they outgrow the mold?
Now they carve out the scars of their branding down to
the bottom of their soul,
where the roots of the iron have reached out and
hugged their heart, grasped it, unwilling to let go.
Then we pry them off with every scream, every cry, and
every emotion left in our burned bodies.
Until all that's left is a small piece of hope. Clinging to

our sore hearts. And from this hope, we set fire.

A fire to forge our own iron in, a fire to brand our own
bloodline with, a fire to feed.
And so we forge a new Baby Brand, hoping to make this
one a little less painful.
Because a sweet baby shouldn't feel the pain of
branding,
They should only admire the scars, and be thankful.
Because they felt no pain.

We have branded our Babies because we have thought
it to be right. Why wouldn't it be?
We seek to save ourselves from the impending storm.
Hoping for them to save us.
And as Babies, we do. Because being brandless is being
branded with no brand.
Now, insurrection is the fire in which our iron is being
forged.
These Branded Babies of Branded Babies, now brand-
ing their own babies.

— Alexis U.
11th Grade

I Am

I am bright
I wonder how far my thoughts in my mind will go
I hear tiny voices in my head telling me to go on
I see my future in signs across the street
I want to never stop with how far I have come
I am bright

I pretend to be okay, though I am better
I feel loved, and I am just enough
I touch the softness of my bed
I worry from time to time about my loved ones
I cry to the sound of depressing songs in the back-
ground filling my ears
I am bright

I understand about the way life goes
I say I will make through anything and everything
I dream nothing but the best for me and my loved ones
I try to please my parents and family members with my
hardworking grades
I hope all of my life is filled with learning and solution
I am bright

— Katina B.
10th grade

They Love Me...
They Love Me Not...

A lotus's curling petals
Kisses the essence of darkness
While shadows tell of plums
Dancing in far away distance

They retreat within each other
As the harrowing claustrophobia
Harms the mind as ours
Pleading, they fight the chaos

From underneath the bud
Invades a growing desire
Piercing through the bottom
Snaps the dragon

A lotus's falling petals
Persevere little me, soon
Little you, too, will bloom into pretty
Snapdragon

— Caroline A.
12th grade

And All the World Starts to Die

Plumes of fire and smoke
paint the sky with fear.
Shots ring out and pierce the silence,
until nothing is left but the lost and the dead.
All around are supporters, condemning the actions
of one and the actions of many.
Few act to save, but those that do,
are the saints from passages long history,
that told tales of the great
who would sacrifice for
those that were sacrificed;
The innocent, the children,
the guilty, the proud,
the ones we remember when
the dust now has cleared.
But before comes the end,
the staggering peace, the faltering
cry to save who is left, is-
Tyranny, bitter power gone
mad, discriminates not against
the opposition or the opposed.
Tyranny, angry and hungry
and hunting, will chase down
the foes and make wreaths
of their bones.
Tyranny, in all of its horror and
crime, will feast on the ashes of
all that was great, and leave in
its wake not a shred of remorse.
So humanity, as often retold by
Hobbes, is at heart only selfish; a
species of animalistic cruelty and

greed. And all we've ever done is prove it
true; subjugation and massacres and
persecution and hate, day in and day out
with no ceasing end. And the very idea
proposed to save us, the solution old
Hobbes wanted for us all, is the
people in charge, the ones leading the
hunt. The same people who would
jump at the chance, to invade, call it home,
and send good people packing.
So now there is tyranny loose in the streets,
now the bodies are piling and the people
are dying, but tyranny has made its home
in the ranks, so now we all pay for the
greed of a few. The innocent, the children,
the guilty, the proud, the ones we remember
and the ones we forgot, are all left in the fires
and ashes and smoke, left to pick up the
pieces and let power corrupt. They
sacrifice and are sacrificed and they falter
in their resolve, because it matters, in the
end, where the real power lies, and when
that power's gone mad, all the world starts to
die.

— Leila I.
10th Grade

Beauty Is In The Eyes

Beauty is in the eye of the beholden
in the flame only just protected
by a hand already littered with scars
in a crow's feet
hanging happily upside down
from sagging cheeks
in a toe that taps
even when it's mostly numb
that which is not indebted
preserved by a gift

— Sydney L.
10th Grade

Traveler

I am looking down at my sleeping body,
hovering above it like a ghost
I wonder where I'm gonna go from here
I hear the taxis swerving past
and the quiet chirp of the country
I see the Hollywood of my mind
and the brick facades of academia
I want...so many things
I am on a ledge-- one that branches from the woods to
high heaven--but it is still a ledge

I pretend the plan is chiseled into my mind
-- by a secret artist who endearingly can never decide
I feel tired of this way pulling and that way pulling
I touch one dream, enough to breathe it in,
before it sours right there in my nose

I worry the artist is not so endearing anymore
I cry only when I'm alone, or else very quietly
I am looking at my paths-- don't look down, don't look
up-- and I can't move

I understand, suddenly,
how quiet the world can be at night
I say softly in my sleep, "hello",
to all the other suspended people,
their hair floating out around their faces
I dream so often, you'd think I'd be better at it,
you'd think it'd feel real
I try to protect them
I hope the falling will stop soon,
 that one of the many colored parachutes will catch
I am weary, traveling while stationary

— Sydney L.
10th Grade

Falling Out of Love

Falling out of love burns.
Like a spoonful of hot sauce.
Then forced to swallow it...
Falling out of love burns like
A sore throat.
Scraping at your vocal cords
As hard swallows drip down your neck.
Falling out of love
Tastes like burnt sugar cookies, hard and crumbly.
Chipping a tooth attempting to take a bite,
Trying not to spit it out.
Falling out of love feels like wet grass.
The morning dew
Seeping into your shorts,
Your bottom, now soggy and cold.
Trying to dust it off, but the dampness doesn't go away.
Falling out of love is like untied shoelaces
Entangling themselves between your ankles,
Dragging you to the concrete.
Skinning your knees and scraping your hands.
Falling out of loves feel like burning your tongue on
scorching soup, Charing your tastebuds.
Preventing you from enjoying your favorite foods.
Replacing their flavors with tastelessness.
Falling out of love
Lingers like sorrowful clouds,
Depositing onto unsuspecting
Tuesday afternoons,
Creeping around the sun
Until Wednesday comes.
But Wednesday brings thunder now.
Falling out of love hurts.

Like broken promises and golden lies.
Wincing at the words, you know aren't real.
Stopped believing now,
But not brave enough to bear the burden of a broken
heart.
Falling out of love
Doesn't draw blood,
It doesn't break skin.
It only leaves bruises.
Sore and small.
Falling out of love burns.
Like a spoonful of hot sauce.
Then forced to swallow it...

— Tara B.
9th Grade

I Am

I am the child of the boulevard of broken dreams,
dreams forgotten to the reality of life.
I wonder why we wish and ponder the ideas of the fu-
ture and never truly execute the solutions to those?
I hear the fear that lingers in the minds and hearts of
those too timid to speak their voices and let their ideas
be heard.
I want a future where little girls can do what they want
without ridicule, where little boys can do what they
wish without ridicule.
I want a future where being human is not something we
judge one another for.
I am the voice of the brokenhearted too timid to speak
their voices, I am the child of the boulevard of broken
dreams.

I pretend to be a god, above all, unharmed by words,
unharmed by the stares. I pretend to be a voice when I
do not even have a voice of my own just yet.
I feel the pain of the sad, the sorrowful, sentimental
bunch, who have yet to find what truly is their beam of
dreams, the beam to lift them to the world and let the
be free.
I touch the minds of those who doubt me, those who
put me down, those who fight against me with a mind
that is not like another.
I worry for the little boys and little girls, who have been
raised like little soldiers who march to a set beat and
not the beat of their own hearts.
I cry for the sad, I cry for the strong, I cry for all those
who have never sung my song, a song to the young a

song to the old. I preach my song till my story is told
I am the string, I am the brave, I come from the
world of broken homes, and I am the child of the
boulevard of broken dreams

I understand your words, I understand your worry,
your worry for the child who is not yours but raised
as your own. I wish for you to see that my path is for
me, so please don't worry
I say to those who seem to push my heart away to
push my mind away to those who tell me to stay si-
lent and smile because that is what little girls do, the
subservient, obedient little girls do.
I dream of a world where being a woman is not a tar-
get, where being black is not a target where being gay
is not a target where being yourself is not a target.
I try to say my words but I may be shushed by the
elders because that is not lady-like. No not ladylike
to speak my mind.
I hope to no longer be defined by my financial situ-
ation, be defined by the color of my skin because I
am not enough for you, I wish not to be defined by
the way you see me I hope to be defined by what you
hear from me.
I am the child of the boulevard of broken dreams, but
I wish to not be defined by that no longer.

— Michaela S.
11th Grade

I Wanna Go Back

I wanna go back to the time
where I was very happy and naive,
with no worries at all

Being outside with friends until the streetlight came on,
heading home after having the time of my life

The laughter and love shared between
my small community as summer
rolled in and school was out
Showing off my new bike to my friends
as we raced each other around the neighborhood with-
out a care in the world
Celebrating my birthday with my community
as a whole like one big happy family

Hearing the sound of the bell
from the man who walked around selling ice cream
I remember the taste of each sweet flavor I ever tried
I remember the bright and beaming smile the man and
I gave to each other

The ability to remember this part of my childhood
is so precious to me

I reminisce a lot about if my childhood best friends
from my old neighborhood remember me, It would
bring me joy to know they are doing great things with
life

Getting home from school every day to go straight to
my best friend's house was sometimes the best part of
my day

Just walking straight into their house because I was no longer just a best friend, I was now part of their family

Having a good childhood is so important in one's life, it's probably the happiest part to reminisce back to

— Kabreyia W.
11th Grade

Changing Periods

Days are changing
The sun sets
Time moves forward
And hardships become unmet

Don't waste your time
Feel it come together
Life changes
And life gets harder

It's harder without them, isn't it?
When the hours get longer, and minutes become like
days
You don't know what to do
And your emotions phase to gray

It's changed once again
And it's not going back
Don't beg for them to stay
Embrace their impact

It's an empty shadow waiting to be filled
Don't stand there halted
Continue your journey
And become who you feel

— Laura K.
11th Grade

A Cat's Affection

Oh, cat paws
The tiny grabs of love
How they help you pounce from above
The tugs of playfulness
Heal some wounds dug

Laying down
I feel you crawl to me
The same process of biscuit making
They knead into my skin like unbaked dough
It warms me up and calms you down

Each little paw
Has a small toe
A bean, if you so
Such a soft touch
Brushing them is a must

Your fluffy greeting is quaint
The calm paw on my leg as awareness
Your nails can dig, but they choose happiness

— Laura K.
11th Grade

That one tear in the wall looms,
that time I was messin' round here.
Pitted down too long, see my expression arid,
touched with a frown here.

I dwell in my capsule, tangible nonsense strewn about.
If you can't bring me wellness,
don't truck and plow here.

Etched in these bricks be scribbles and scrawls,
lack of stimuli makes it not all that profound here.

Tomorrow is yesterday and was
the other day Thursday?
Confused, perplexed,
oh how the doctrine so blurry and unsound here.

Max, tell me what you see outside.
I plead! Permit my freedom. I'm beyond wounded here.

— Max L.
10th Grade

O Music

Singing softly in the shine
For once blinded by the light

The world zooms out, stops
Yet I'm still right there and time skips and hops
Painfully aware and happily somewhere else
All at once

It's a story, it's a shot of what the world should be, no filler
It is mine, then it's everyone's to almost see
A gift given to the world, given by it
Which costs nothing

But can I borrow your ear for a minute?

— Payton L.
11th Grade

Ode to Coffee

Jealous of the way You always make me feel alive
Like a star that hasn't stopped burning
Or maybe it has, and we just don't know it yet.
And you're never the same thing twice
There's hints of change, signs, almost
Sweet one moment, bitter the next
Because we've changed the recipe, every time
 You keep me awake Even when I don't want to be
You give me energy
 When I've used it all up.
That dark hazy brown keeps me warm
Makes me feel at home
 And though it burns sometimes, I can't function with-
out it.
 And soon I'm out of coffee
Tea is a temporary replacement
Cause even though it's warm and sweet, It isn't you

— Hollen H.
12th Grade

Roll Call for the Missing Piece

You remind me of things that I'm glad I forgot
Things that still writhe inside me
Which reminds me why I needed that reminder
He kicked me in the head at the starting line
And left me to finish the race
Even once the bleeding stopped, I couldn't really
see right
Because there was blood on my face
And my teeth hurt
And my legs seemed to move awkwardly
Inexplicably different from their track-star running
And people change over this much time
I can't hate him now, I don't know him
And I can't remember the starting line
But I remember the kick
It's always happening somewhere

— Payton L.
11th Grade

Ode to my Shoes

My dearest valentines shoes.
Wandering around the world
Adorned with tiny
Red
Embroidered
Hearts.
Dancing along the frame of your body.
My dearest valentine shoes
Your flushed pink soles
Wandering around the world
Like skipping through pools of
Candy
Conversation
Hearts.
My dearest valentines shoes
Your blushing pink secrets.
Hidden under my feet.
Wandering around the world
Like playing hop-scotch
On
cotton
candy
cement
The squares, drawn with bubble gum chalk.
My dearest valentine shoes.
Wandering around the world.
Standing two inches taller.
Your platform lifts me to
the woven wool clouds
Pirouetting through the sky.
Painting
Purple

Promises for a new day
Gently along the evening sunset.
My dearest valentines shoes
Hugging my ankles tight,
Wandering around the world
Like holding hands while
Frolicking through
The forbidden buds
Of Forget Me Nots.

— Tara B.
9th Grade

Ode to Spiders

Those gorgeous webs spun on the wall
Is where you'll find someone quite small,
Whom many loathe, despise, detest;
But I will do my very best
To state their case and just request
A change in the minds of all.
The bugs we humans love to hate
Are food for those whose legs count eight.
Whatever we consider pests;
Mosquitoes, flies, and all the rest,
Are often spiders' dinner guests
And end up on the plate!
Beauty is subjective, sure
But no manner of preference can obscure
The sheen of a spider's many eyes
Or the gracile legs, of any size;
And surely no-one can deny
The spider's skilled couture!
Their webs, of course! That's their whole thing;
Of silken constructs, they're the kings!
A web festooned with morning dew
Is such an extraordinary view.
And so I know that one thing's true;
Spiders are masters of string.
I sing the praises of spiders clear;
For these little creatures I hold dear.
However, despite their many charms,
Many only wish spiders harm!
I promise you, though; there's no cause for alarm.
Such spider slander's a smear.
So when it comes to spiders, I recommend
That we all try to make amends.

Next time, when you see a spinner
Waiting on its web for dinner,
See the beauty just within her;
For spiders are our friends.

— Parker Y.
12th Grade

Then - Soon - Now

I am saddened by all that we will never know,
that we cannot know;
I wonder how much has been lost to time forever;
Never will
I hear the sound of our ancestors' bone-flutes,
sounded around the camp-fire; Never will
I see the colors of Roman statues, painted vividly in
antiquity but now drab.
I want to know what lies beyond the veil of history,
and of prehistory, for
I am curious...

I pretend that something may exist beyond what we
now know.
I feel awed by the possibilities of life beyond Earth, and
dream that someday may
I touch the surface of another planet, soon to be a new
home for hairless apes.
I worry, though, for our own dying space rock.
I cry, desperately realizing that the Final Frontier mat-
ters more to some than our First;
I am embarrassed that other intelligences might witness
our planetary negligence and scoff in disgust.

I understand, though, what we know now.
I say, "We can't let ambition cloud our eyes. We must
fix what we have broken. We must have patience."
I dream of a distant humanity spread across multiple,
healthy planets.
I try to help others understand.
I hope they can.
I am optimistic.

— Parker Y.
12th Grade

Prescription Bottles

Another long name I won't remember
Another milliliter I have to remember
The taste aches me
The flavors gag me

Don't take too much
Don't take too little
Will it matter?
I won't dwindle

What do I have
Why do I break
I keep coughing and coughing
Is it a mistake

Is it my own game
Let the battery drain
Down my hand
Your needle pierced my arm
I cant stand

This is different for me
But others are used to it
2 puffs in
Let it all out
Make sure to count to 10
Or you'll let it out

— Laura K.
11th Grade

The Folds of Energy

It is but a fact that god is in here
but simultaneously beside this world
yet gone from this place curled
up within a ball of yarn, lace, and disease.

God is not a god but a substance, and thus substance is
god
but this is a substance surrounding all?
For this I can only speculate, my reason being crawled
from the depths of the mind, and from the lengths of
the tall
violence which seeps down into us all.

Down beyond the smallest atom, the quarks, and the
strings
lay the groundwork for energy and pure substance of
the universal.
He who brings all of the things throughout the beings
is founded in this place of all folds and transversals.
And this is where the curves emerge.

For they fold, the folding of things on top of things
is the real motion. It is not difference. No, no, no.
The breeze atop the trees is not separate from the wings
of branches which it folds to and fro.
And this is where the curves take shape.

For they concentrate into shapes and move away from
abstractions.
But the abstractions are only within our own creation,
so we then must ask: "what are your true actions?".
So the substance goes, and energy formations
form intensities and condensations.

Am I speaking rationally?
Can you understand my voice?

It may not be the correction of language that must change but
rather your own articulation of thought. Think of the gut.
The seemingly non-liner structure of the intestine forms its structure
as a multi-dimensional formation, for he exists in whole as rupture.
Shapes and identities who come from this are merely condensations
of the substance in a body of organization, territorializations.

My lips are merely speaking in twofold articulation
from my own truth, my unguarded figuration
the lips who line the opening of my mouth,
for they project all, but not south.
No, not at all, for he who seeks this
must become one step away from novice
of my speech. For its language is clear as it can be.
One must only look for it to find the simplicity.

Organization, intensities, matters who are all one.
Oh my! This sounds like so much fun!
But these organizations and vessels of the substances are one.
I've told you time and time again, and I will continue
to do so until you become sick of the monotony.
All of the avenues for which energy can take, taken anew,
merely seem that they are separate spaces.

But on closer examination they are all still the same.
The same thing, the same but only less and more con-
centrated.
Air is the allusion of freedom from the substance,
when in reality, it may just be the substance in its least
contortion.
(It is space who's substance may even be considered
stretched out!)
And this is where the energy folds.

For it is only a quasi-multidimensional formation
whom
concentrates like the gravitational womb
of wells and bodies who concentrate the fabrics of
space-time
the fabrics are really just a gel who condense with the
chime
of closed proximity
And these energy folds morph.

They emerge as condensations of bodies who's reality
is the same as every other as each of them actually
connected by their mere quality of existence
as quantum foams noting their resistance
to anything that attempts to sever
themselves from the foundational ever
eternal substance, for this may only require energy
and as we know: energy is substance at its primal

And we know that any energy attempting to cleave
itself from its others is only an attempt to leave
apart of its own self from the rest of itself.
But it needs itself to leave itself?
What a strange occurrence.

But I say "No! Energy cannot leave at all!
Energy is all and for all it shall fall,
to one day be known to stand tall
above the rest and only on the chest
of those on their own selves, for this is all we do!"

There is no process which is not done directly to ourselves.
Yet each process may be directly and indirectly to our
specific conscious bodies.
But these bodies then raise the question of consciousness.
Good lord, have we found ourselves upon the roughness
of questions, and for now we can just say that consciousness
exists merely as unknown of its other parts and it can
only be of its own
condensation on other bodies who's self is by the seas of
the bones.

And with this in mind, we may continue further.
The notations of the biosphere, technosphere,
and all spheres that continue
are separated and disjointed
by our own social implications, affected and connected
through our retroactive articulation of ideas.

The gel who condenses in certain areas cannot break
itself off from itself, it is as if a piece of this gel
tried to make itself differentiated in a pool of itself
screaming and trying to produce a yell
that can only be heard by itself, and the ones that take
the severed section back into itself.

With all this in mind, we maybe can establish

some sort of model of deterritorialization,
some method which we can use to flourish.
But this takes under a great confusion, coordination
will be immensely hindered.
And it is here where the energy folds unto their selves.

Bodies without organs? No, maybe.
These, or this, structure modifies into
realms of revolving themselves, these revolutions
are turned merely by folding and pushing
and stretching.

Stars. Our stars. The stars are products of the conden-
sations
who have had themselves forced in so much that they
turn pure.
In only by their certain connotations,
do the condensations end up forming knots so extreme
and sure
that they are in control that they expand so far out.
And our energy can then explain so much.

Wormholes. Black holes.
And machines of information deletion.
All of which occur on the error of the energy.
Whereas energy as a universal substance relies upon
the destination
of its inability to be broken off,
there is the susceptibility
for it to have the ability of the energy to be torn.
Ruptures and expositions of the information
before it is entered.
A hole in a connection with other openings w
ho then form tubes,
are formed through the early stages of substance.
And from energy everything rises.

— Thomas B.
11th Grade

WHITESVILLE ELEMENTARY

TEACHERS: MS. HICKS AND MS. LEGETTE
POET INSTRUCTOR: YVETTE MURRAY
5TH GRADE

Here in the dawn, hearing
The horse chatter.
Winter months feel so cold.
Yeah I'm standing out here all
Alone. Looking down at the jasper
Leaves and trees look so cold.
Looking up at the cerulean sky,
Reflecting back on my life.
When I see my friends playing I wish I was there.
If only I could
I wish I would.

— Allie S.
5th Grade

One fall night, it was lofty and the leaves feel softly.
The wind was cool, and the sky was blue.
The clouds were fluffy and grass was tuffy
Many leaves on the ground. With the chiffon winter
nearing
While I lie down in my cozy little tent!
And so I fell asleep once more.
While holding my sleeping bag held tight.
Dreaming of the fall morning.

— Arianna H.
5th Grade

As fall had awoken the other seasons fall, the bright
beautiful vermilion color spread over the fall, all the
other seasons fall, fall my seasons fall! :> :)

— Chelsea H.
5th Grade

Winter

Footprints left in the snow whole
I walk across the lawn.
Shoveling all the snow away so we can go and park
Not getting bit by bugs because they have gone and died

— Benjamin M.
5th Grade

On the beautiful summer day the wind blew my away
I saw the elegant birds fly by which gives me a big smile
on my face and my makes my heart race I see the serene
flowers that are green
While the bees sing by I feel more and more okay on
this beautiful summer day

— Donovan A.
5th Grade

Fall is chill the colors are titian what a wonderful set-
ting for walks and talks come on outside get some nice
fresh air and enjoy this fun fall fair

— Victoria J.
5th Grade

A Silent Story

As the chiffon crystals fall from the cerulean sky the
wood turns from warm to a bisque color

I stand in the middle of the chiffon forest covered in the
light color of snow

I hear the freezing, cracking of the icicles near

Then midnight awakes along with all the creatures

I look towards the obsidian sky, I see fantastic jasper
lights with a small hint of smalt blue.

I soon see an owl swoop down from the tall slender
trees and I hear rodents scurry across the soft cool
ground

Soon I take a calming walk to the cabin on the white hill
surrounded by tall slender trees

Soon I go to bed to have a long slumber, I listen to
the sounds of the crackling fire and the sound of a cat
purring.

I shut my eyes and slowly fall asleep with a cat in arm. :

— Giana B.
5th Grade

Back to Back

Spring is coming, time to play back to back
we will all say.
Rain is back, raindrops falling, and it comes in a big
shower back to back we will all say. Ducks come back
flying, flapping their wings back to back we will all say.
The heat fades, ice on my fingertips back to back we will
all say. Ice melts away again no more snow, for one final
time back to back we will all say.

— Jeanette C.
5th Grade

When I Walk On A Day/Night

When I walk on a winter night
I see the ground is fully white
The snow slowly melts on the granite
When I walk on a winter night

When I walk on a winter day
I see the birds fly away
I hope the snow is here to stay
When I walk on a winter day

When I walk on a summer night
I miss the sun shining bright
I see some owls taking flight
When I walk on a summer night

When I walk on a summer day
All I'll do is play play play
and I'll sing "Hey hey hey!"
When I walk on summer day

— Josiah W.
5th Grade

How I Know It's Spring

I love
The seasons
Because they change
Even though it is a bit strange
As I walk through the leaves I
Will always feel a tiny breeze and
One more thing i like is the bees even
If they do sting as the birds fly i see they're
Wings and now i know spring will begin

— Kadence W.
5th Grade

Fall Oh Fall

Fall means to ball and never to be small.
The tree leaves turn bittersweet
Oh boy is it a treat. Leaves fall down which cause me to
frown.
Fall oh fall this have has come to a haul

— Kayla S.
5th Grade

Seasons Expressing Their True Feelings

The sun shone above the cerulean clouds as the saplings changed colors throughout the seasons, as the trees blew through the wind, the trees were starting to mature. Trees leaves falling on the gloomy day. The seasons were expressing their true feelings. The vines of the trees grew as the fire once did, with colors of the vermilion season of autumn.

— Kaylor M.
5th Grade

A Cold Winter Night

A cold winter night. Looking up you can see the chiffon moon surrounded by the obsidian sky.
Looking at the ground, you can see the chiffon snow and the cerulean ice on the obsidian road, you can hear the quiet footsteps of the people walking the sidewalks and cars going past you.

— Kenneth H.
5th Grade

Fall

The bittersweet leaves glisten in the sunlight
The fall breeze blowing through my fingertips
The ducks flying south towards the warmth while us
in the cold
Soon comes my birthday 11 to be
In the darkness, I will see snow to be

— Mackenzie M.
5th Grade

Most of the time in fall there are bittersweet and
vermilion leaves on the trees.

— Mason D.
5th Grade

The leaves of bittersweet make the drums beat .The
wind of fall make the bells tall. The footsteps of the
fiery leaves flow through my fingertips
And I feel fall's rhythm coming out my lips. The eyes
of the sleeping forest of falls light make my spirit
bright. The touch of falls love makes my heart go
THUMP THUMP. These words dump fall's rhythm
on the tips of your thumb.

— Persephone M.
5th Grade

Mother Winter

The wind was crisp and cold. My fingers felt like ice. It felt like I had just got a kiss on the cheek from Mother Winter. There were Pansies blooming all around. The dark black forest made it feel like I was in a cage of trees slowly closing in on me yet it felt warming. The snow crunches beneath my snow boots and the sound makes my heart happy. Even though it is harsh and cold, I still love winter.

— Riley H.
5th Grade

As the seasons change new fruits grow, once fall comes it's time to go to pumpkin row now be careful of the new found thorns they might cut you and leave you to mourn

— Robert S.
5th Grade

A Mixed Season

A mixed season there was, a day of joy and a day of fun.
It was cold and warm. The clouds came out and they
were very white. It started snowing even when the sun
shined.
And there was a girl that was full of excitement. As the
sun still shined it was warm outside
it felt like summer and winter at the same time.
 I thought I was dreaming at night. As the people played
in snow they were wearing summer clothes.
THERE WAS A MIXED SEASON.

— Brantley B.
5th Grade

Fall is my Favorite Season

Trees are changing, leaves are falling silent.
Nights get longer, as days get shorter. Fall seems short
but Halloween is long. Fall is over but Halloween is
never. Winter is here, Christmas is coming. When fall
ends winter starts but fall will always be my favorite
season.

— Delaney V.
5th Grade

Fall

Leaves crunching below my feet
I wish I could have gotten more sleep
Fall is the best time of year
Especially because Fall is full of fear
But sometimes I think about the leaves
How they live, grow and fall
All night long
But i won't waste my time on that
So I can go inside and take a nap.

— Katelyn O.
5th Grade

I love a season that's not the best.... i guess! The season
that I like rhymes with bummer it's summer. I guess
you could guess that it was summer or not. It was not
the best season but it was something. I like summer
because it's hot and i have a pool that's like a pot and
it's not that hot

— Haven S.
5th Grade

I Love Spring

I love spring. I love how it is not so freezing cold but
not so burning hot. I love the smalt sky. I love it when it
rains and I look at it through my window.

— London H.
5th Grade

On sunny mornings I go outside to lay on jasper grass. I like to brake the vermilion leaves and shake the trees. I like to go swimming in the cerulean water and splash people. I like to play with my damask dogs. I also like to jump on the obsidian trampoline. These are things I like to do on a sunny summer day.

I like to lay on the jasper grass and look up at the cerulean sky. I like to roll down the hill. I like to cut the jasper grass. I like to jump on the jasper grass. I like to kick the jasper grass. That's what I like to do with jasper grass.

I like to blow the vermilion leaves off the jasper grass. I like to climb the trees so the vermilion leaves can fall off on the jasper grass. I like to hang on the tree and the vermilion leaves. I like to shake the tree so the vermilion leaves fall off. I like to kick the tree so the vermilion leaves fall off. That what i do to tree

I like to dive into the cerulean pool. I like to swim under the water. I like to jump in the cerulean pool. I like to do a belly flop in the cerulean pool. I like to play pool games. That's what I like to do in the cerulean pool.

The damask dog can be crazy some days so i have to put the damask dog in the sepia cage. I like to take my damask dogs on a walk. I like to give my damask dogs puce treats if they learn tricks. I love to sleep with my damask dogs on my titian couch. I like to clean the dogs. That is what I do to my dogs.

I like to do front flips on the obsidian trampoline. I like to do backflips on the obsidian trampoline. I like to do

jumping cartwheels on the obsidian trampoline. I like
to do exercise on the obsidian trampoline. I like to do
jumping jacks on the obsidian trampoline. That is what
I like to do on my obsidian trampoline.

— Jailyn C.
5th Grade

Moon On Halloween

Tonight is my favorite night tonight
I shine my beams on children tossed
In twilight dressed up in nighttime dreams
Tonight from home to home they go. Tonight
Light their way. Tonight the world holds magic.
It will be gone by day.

— Landon H.
5th Grade

Time in the Winter

The times in the winter, the time in my life
It is such a day to have a good time.
Watching movies with hot chocolate in my hands,
I wish this day would never end.
Laughing and giggling with my family,
Around this time we have a lot of empathy.

Going outside to skate all day long,
Have fun all day and singing some songs.
We all feel the warmness of the bonfire,
All year this was something we desired.
Now we get to have warm drinks,
So many things that we love to thank.
Being excited when Christmas comes around.
Seeing decorations all around town.
Wearing thick jackets so we can be warm,
Buying new decorations from the store.
This is the time of my life.

—Gianna E.
5th Grade

The Spring is amazing and it's only 3 days and you can
even go on vacation
Last spring i went to Myrtle Beach and it was fun. The
spring is like summer but only
3 days. So yeah the spring is also a hot when its, spring
its, even more FUN outside.

— Landon B.
5th Grade

Poets in
Schools

www.ingramcontent.com/pod-product-compliance
Lightning Source LLC
Chambersburg PA
CBHW062056080426
42734CB00012B/2666